The Andrew R. Cecil Lectures on

Moral Values in a Free Society

established by

The University of Texas at Dallas

Volume XVII

Previous Volumes of the Andrew R. Cecil Lectures
on Moral Values in a Free Society

MORAL VALUES: THE CHALLENGE OF THE TWENTY-FIRST CENTURY

Moral Values: The Challenge of the Twenty-First Century

ANDREW R.CECIL
GLENN C. LOURY
JOHN WITTE, JR.
JOANNE B. CIULLA
BRUCE JENNINGS

With an Introduction by
ANDREW R. CECIL

Edited by
W. LAWSON TAITTE

The University of Texas at Dallas
1996

FOREWORD

The Andrew R. Cecil Lectures on Moral Values in a Free Society were established by the University of Texas at Dallas in 1979 to provide a forum for the discussion of vital issues confronting our society. During each subsequent November, U.T. Dallas has invited to its campus scholars, businessmen and members of the professions, public officials, and other notable individuals to share their ideas on a theme related to this subject with the academic community and the general public. During the seventeen years of their existence, the Cecil Lectures have become a valued tradition for the University and for the wider community. The presentations of the many distinguished authorities who have participated in the program have enriched the experience of all those who heard them or read the published proceedings of each series. They have enlarged our understanding of the system of moral values on which our country was founded and continues to rest.

The University named this program for Dr. Andrew R. Cecil, its Distinguished Scholar in Residence. During his tenure as President of The Southwestern Legal Foundation, Dr. Cecil's innovative leadership brought that institution into the forefront of continuing legal education in the United States. When he retired from the Foundation as its Chancellor Emeritus, Dr. Cecil was asked by U.T. Dallas to serve as its Distinguished Scholar in Residence, and the Cecil Lectures were instituted. In 1990, the Board of Regents of The University of Texas System established the Andrew R. Cecil Chair of Applied Ethics. It is appropriate that the Lectures and the Chair honor a man who has been concerned throughout his career with the moral foundations of our society and has stressed his belief in the dignity and worth of every individual.

The seventeenth annual series of the Cecil Lectures was held on the University's campus on November 6 through 8, 1995. It examined the theme of "Moral Values: The Challenge of the Twenty-First Century." On behalf of U.T. Dallas, I would like to express our appreciation to Professor Glenn C. Loury, Professor John Witte, Jr., Professor Joanne B. Ciulla, Mr. Bruce Jennings, and Dr. Cecil for their willingness to share their ideas and for the outstanding lectures that are preserved in this volume of proceedings.

This is also an opportunity to express on behalf of the University our deep appreciation to all those who have helped make this program an important part of the life of the University, especially the contributors to the Lectures. Through their support, these donors enable us to continue this important program and to publish the proceedings of the series, thus assuring a wide and permanent audience for the ideas the books contain.

I am confident that everyone who reads *Moral Values: The Challenge of the Twenty-First Century*, the Andrew R. Cecil Lectures on Moral Values in a Free Society Volume XVII, will be stimulated by the ideas expressed there so eloquently.

FRANKLYN G. JENIFER, President
The University of Texas at Dallas
February 1996

CONTENTS

INTRODUCTION

by

Andrew R. Cecil

As we approach a new century, our society's pride in the achievements of our own time—especially the extraordinary growth of scientific knowledge and the related explosion of technological capabilities—is coupled with a pervading anxiety about the future. The growth of the world's population, the shortage of resources, our decaying cities, the disarray of the international political and economic system, troublesome environmental problems, the threat of nuclear war—these are only some of the world's problems that have piled up, unresolved by the technological achievements of the current century.

In the United States, we try to comfort ourselves with the belief that this country, as the leading world power and industrial democracy, is different from the rest of the world—that we have solved our day-to-day problems. Such optimism—undergirded with the best of intentions—obscures the reality of the social problems that remain among us. To name only a few, these include violence, drugs, and other

13

crime; illiteracy, homelessness, and poverty; and the rising rate of illegitimacy in our society.

A vigorous debate over these issues, which are of such pressing concern, is taking place now in our country. It largely concerns the means we should use to address them: What is the proper role of the government in solving these problems without depriving individuals of their right to shape their own destinies?

Let us take, for example, the issue of social welfare. In the democracies of Europe, in Canada, and in the United States, the welfare systems are under an enormous strain. Increases in life expectancy continue to push spending on welfare upward—an aging population has a large impact on publicly provided pensions and health care. Welfare spending by federal, state, and local governments in the United States from 1988 through 1992 increased from $217 billion to $305 billion. The "welfare state" providing support "from the cradle to the grave" has fallen into disrepute, and the political pressure for fundamental reform of the welfare system is gaining strength and popularity.

Because some of the social policies of the national government unwisely nourished a culture of dependency, there is a trend to shift the responsibility for solving our social problems to state and local governments. The idea of moving strong nongovernmental institutions to the front lines in tempering and restraining the behaviors causing our social ills also has its advocates. Among them is Charles Murray, the author of the book *Losing Ground*, who sees in illegitimacy the most important social problem of our time. He strongly suggests that a single mother who wants to keep a child should not expect subsidies from the government but should enlist support from parents, boyfriend, siblings, neighbors, churches, and philanthropies. Furthermore, since the act of having an illegitimate child is profoundly irresponsible, the need to find support from other sources than the government will, according to Murray, regenerate the stigma that single parenthood carried in the past. ("The Coming White Underclass," *The Wall Street Journal*, October 29, 1993, p. A14.)

On the same note, *Newsweek* suggests that "Americans are fed up with everything from teen pregnancy to drunk drivers." In order to restore the lost sense of right and wrong, the article calls for "the return of shame" and claims that shame has begun to shove itself back into our late-twentieth-century consciousness. It represents itself in our "anger over crime, welfare, politicians" and on occasion in the guilty person's "remorse, even mortification." (Jonathan Adler and Pat Wingert, "The Return of Shame," *Newsweek*, February 6, 1995, p. 21.)

A widespread necessity to impose stigma or shame, the feeling of disgrace arising from the consciousness of having done something dishonorable, is a mark of social degeneration. What kind of degeneration and disgrace are we facing? The answer is a decay of moral standards, which has caused the confusion and moral uncertainty that attend our efforts in finding solutions to the social evils facing us. This decay of moral values demands their restoration. Moral recovery will take place not by building more prisons or more orphanages for illegitimate children but by restoring the national conscience that determines the social and moral values of our society.

Conscience plays an important part in determining the role and scope of morality in private and public life. To the British philosopher Anthony Cooper, Lord Shaftesbury (1671-1713), is attributed the term "moral sense"—man's natural sense of right and wrong in a universe which is essentially harmonious. His ideas were followed by Francis Hutcheson (1694-1746), a professor of moral philosophy at the University of Glasgow, who in his "benevolent theory" of moral conduct argued that satisfaction from virtuous and benevolent behavior arises not from the benefits it brings to the one who practices it but from the beauty and merits of the act itself. Shaftesbury, Hutcheson, and other philosophers maintained that moral ideas are innate in man, that man possesses an "inborn sense" that enables him to discern moral values.

The moral sense may differ in degree in individual members of society and in different societies, but no reasonable being, whether controlled by it or not in his conduct, is wholly destitute of it. As conscience was once described by our courts: "Greatly enlightened it is in some by reason of superior education, quickened in others because of settled religious belief in future accountability, dulled in others by vicious habits, but never altogether absent in any." (*Miller v. Miller*, 41 A. 277, 280, 187 Pa. 572 [1898].) It is our responsibility to eradicate such "vicious habits" and to inculcate an adherence to generally prevailing standards of right conduct that enhance a nation's well-being.

What kind of conduct will enhance our nation's well-being in the forthcoming century? In my lecture on "Moral Values or the Will to Power," I try to seek an answer to this overwhelming question, which transcends mere technical or economic development: In the forthcoming century, will morality be the dominant force, or will the new century extol power for its own sake in a world divorced from ethical principles? The issue is whether the principles of morality formulated by Kant as the "categorical imperative" and epitomized by the spirit of the Gospel are adopted or the new century turns to a philosophy of power, such as the one formulated by Nietzsche, that sees strength as the ultimate virtue. This is the great challenge to be faced by the new millennium.

One of the maladies of the end of this century is the decline of the middle class and the growing distance between the small "overclass" (increasingly gathering more and more of society's wealth and income) and the growing "underclass" (isolated from sources of income and wealth). Such a division is not conducive to social cohesion. Aristotle stressed the importance of the middle class by pointing out that it "has a great steadying influence and checks the opposing extremes" of the rich and the poor.

When we think about welfare programs, we think not about the downtrodden but about lazy people getting assistance they do not deserve. When we think of starving people, we think about Somalia, Rwanda, or other Third World countries and not about the United States—where in October 1995 the U.S. Census Bureau acknowledged that 38 million Americans, or about 14.5 percent of our population, lived in poverty in 1994. (The Commerce Department set the official poverty level in 1994 as $15,141 annual income for a family of four.)

Compassion for the poor has been a mark of the Judaeo-Christian tradition. Poverty is ethically intolerable. The Old Testament expresses God's concern for the poor: "And if he cries to me, I will hear, for I am compassionate." (Exodus 22:27.) Amos condemns the people of Israel because they "trample the head of the poor into the dust of the earth, and turn aside the way of the afflicted." (Amos 2:7.)

Christ's ministry reveals compassion for the hungry, the ill, and the poor. The words of Jesus, "How blessed are you who are poor; the kingdom of God is yours" (Luke 6:20), were not intended to permit us to evade our responsibility but should be seen in the light of the warnings against indifference. "If a brother or sister is ill-clad and in lack of daily food, and one of you says to them 'Go in peace, be warmed and filled,' without giving them the things needed for the body, what does it profit? So faith by itself, if it has no works, is dead." (James 2:15-17.)

The German theologian Dietrich Bonhoeffer, who died at the hands of the Nazis (hanged for treason at the age of 39) and whose voice after his death grew louder than ever in martyrdom, believed that the church should give its wealth to the poor. Improving the lives of the poor on earth, he maintained, is of equal importance with saving souls for heaven.

Confucius once wrote: "It is harder to be poor without murmuring than to be rich without arrogance." In the poor and the hungry, there is an undercurrent of hostility toward those who possess and enjoy abundance and plenty. A Spanish proverb says: "Quien ha criados ha enemigos no escusados" (he who has servants has unavoidable enemies).

Poverty has particularly affected the lives of racial or ethnic minorities. The large number of ethnic minorities that this country has welcomed makes us what President John F. Kennedy called "this nation of immigrants." For more than two centuries of our history, it has been the American dream that this vast array of cultures and heritages should somehow blend into one new entity. The American dream has been to become the "melting pot" in which a multitude of ethnic and cultural identities are fused into a single nation. This dream, however, has never been fully realized.

Racism has always been, and still remains, inconsistent with equality of rights as they pertain to citizenship and with the personal liberty which ought to be enjoyed within this free land of ours. Efforts toward the abolishment of racism in our institutions were made by the Thirteenth and Fourteenth Amendments. The Thirteenth Amendment was adopted to strike down the institutions of slavery and involuntary service everywhere in the United States. It was followed by the Fourteenth Amendment, which was adopted to ensure that every person must be treated equally by each state regardless of the color of his skin. Almost a century passed before the states and the federal government were finally directed to eliminate all detrimental classifications based on race.

Justice John Marshall Harlan's dissent in the *Plessy v. Ferguson* case, in which the Court applied

the "separate but equal" doctrine, was a landmark
in the long history of this process. "If," stated the
Court's majority opinion, "the civil and political
rights of both races be equal, one cannot be inferior
to the other civilly or politically. If one race is
inferior to the other socially, the Constitution of the
United States cannot put them upon the same
plane." (16 S. Ct. 1138, 1143 [1896].) Justice
Harlan claimed, however, that the Thirteenth and
Fourteenth Amendments decreed universal civil
freedom in this country and removed the race line
from our governmental systems. "The white race
deems itself to be the dominant race in this country," he wrote,

"but in view of the Constitution, in the eye of
the law, there is in this country no superior,
dominant class of citizens. There is no caste
here. Our Constitution is color-blind, and neither
knows nor tolerates classes. In respect of civil
rights, all citizens are equal before the law. The
humblest is the peer of the most powerful. The
law regards man as man, and takes no account of
his surroundings or of his color when the civil
rights as guaranteed by the supreme law of the
land are involved." (*Id.*, at 558.)

After the long dormancy of the Equal Protection
Clause, the Congress and the Supreme Court em-
barked on the crucial mission of assuring to all

persons "the protection of equal laws." The push of equality initiated by the legislative branch of the government was paralleled by decisions in the judicial branch. However, in our search for truth that may be discovered by reason and revelation, we are far from claiming that court decisions or civil rights legislation offer an absolute solution to the problem of race relations in the United States. The question of the highest order is: Can the remedies offered for "historic discrimination" bring minority groups into the mainstream of American life?

Recently an issue that has ignited angry emotions is the debate on the "fairness" of affirmative action. This debate is marked by tension and contradictions. The use of affirmative action for racial and gender preference raises the question whether the Fourteenth Amendment permits preferential treatment as a means of remedying past discrimination. A "preferred" status for a particular racial or ethnic minority entails resentment on the part of persons who are denied equal rights and opportunities on the basis of membership in the "dominant majority."

There is a certain measure of inequity, stated the Supreme Court in the *Bakke* case, in forcing innocent persons to bear the burden of redressing grievances not of their making or to suffer otherwise impermissible burdens in order to enhance the standing of certain ethnic groups. Furthermore, wrote

Justice Lewis Powell, "preferential programs may only reinforce common stereotypes holding that certain groups are unable to achieve success without special protection based on a factor having no relationship to individual worth." (*Bakke v. Regents of the University of California*, 98 S. Ct. 2733, 2752 [1978].)

Do race and gender preferences cause "reverse discrimination"? This question is widely discussed in labor, business, academic, and political circles, as well as by the press. It is also a topic being debated by presidential candidates in the 1996 elections. Some of the candidates aspiring for the White House, in their opposition to racial preferences in employment and college admission, promise to introduce legislation banning racial and gender preferences, which they claim are "patently unfair" and create divisiveness. The advocates of the legacy of affirmative action maintain that it gives minorities and women an opportunity to compete, which is a laudable achievement in a multiracial and multiethnic society.

The divisiveness deepens when affirmative action lapses into a system of quotas in which businesses are urged to establish certain percentages as hiring goals for minorities and women and universities are required to set up similar goals for appointing faculty members and for student admissions.

Professor Glenn C. Loury in his lecture "Individualism Before Multiculturalism" argues that such policies as affirmative action proceed from mistaken assumptions. Finally, they harm the very people they are designed to assist. Professor Loury believes that any definition of the human person that finds its essence in race, class, gender, or any other single characteristic dehumanizes those it seeks to define. Those who define identity in this way divide our society and make peace and unity impossible.

Professor Loury maintains that it is extremely harmful to categorize the results of IQ tests in racial or other such terms. Similarly, poverty and crime should not be seen as racial problems but as human problems. The example of Martin Luther King, Jr., and the other greatest African American leaders has always shown that inclusion within society without regard to race or color should be the goal of all Americans.

This concept of the dignity of every individual, which was the moving force guiding the founders of this country, represented the heritage of their religious faith. Our forefathers stressed the values of independence and self-discipline, but they realized that such qualities emanated from two sources of moral authority transcending all offices and boundaries: the Old and New Testaments.

As I mentioned earlier, our society's responsibility to inculcate adherence to prevailing standards of right conduct must be carried out by restoring our national conscience, which determines the social and moral ideas of our society. Some may have doubts about the success of a moral counterrevolution, but it is worthwhile to try to cast light on the heritage of values instilled in our institutions by our forefathers. Without question, this heritage has religious roots.

Plutarch, the learned Greek historian and biographer, once observed that he had been told of towns which were unfortified, illiterate, or without the conveniences usual to human dwelling places, but that no traveler had ever brought back reports of a people wholly without religion. One might as well seek to erect a city in the air, he believed, as to unify a state where there is no worship of any divinity.

Deep religious convictions—primarily Christian beliefs—guided the founders of the United States. The Declaration of Independence proclaimed the birth of our nation "with a firm reliance on the protection of Divine Providence." George Washington began his inaugural address with "fervent supplication to that Almighty Being who rules over the universe" and in his farewell address besought "the Almighty to avert or mitigate" whatever evils the new republic might face. Abraham Lincoln prayed at Gettysburg "that this nation, under God, shall have a new birth of freedom."

References to our religious heritage are found in the statutorily prescribed national motto, "In God We Trust" and in the Pledge of Allegiance to the American flag, which says that we are "one nation under God." There are countless illustrations of the accommodation of religion in American public life to support the opinion expressed by Justice William O. Douglas that "we are a religious people whose institutions presuppose a Supreme Being."

The religious atmosphere in this country, in the words of Alexis de Tocqueville, the French statesman and writer, "was the first thing that struck" him on his arrival in the United States. In his desire to understand the reason for this phenomenon, he questioned "the faithful of all communions." He particularly sought the society of clergymen, who "are depositories of the various creeds and have a personal interest in their survival." His research convinced him that the "main reason for the quiet sway of religion over their country was the complete separation of church and state. I have no hesitation in stating that throughout my stay in America I met nobody, lay or cleric, who did not agree about that." (*Democracy in America*, trans. by George Lawrence, Harper & Row Publishers, 1966, pp. 271-272.)

Belief in the separation of church and state does not preclude the conviction that religion's moral code bears on our laws and forms an operative part of our social obligation. Our courts throughout the centuries have taken a position that Christianity has entered and influenced, more or less, all our institutions, customs, and relations, as well as our individual modes of thinking and acting.

"It is so involved in our social nature, that even those among us who reject Christianity cannot possibly get clear of its influence, or reject those sentiments, customs and principles which it has spread among the people, so that, like the air we breathe, they have become the common stock of the whole country, and essential elements of its life." (*Mohney v. Cook*, 26 Pa. 342 [1855].)

More than a century later, the Supreme Court again acknowledged the role of religion in American life. In *Lynch v. Donnelly* in March 1984, for instance, the Supreme Court held that the Constitution does not require complete separation of church and state; it affirmatively mandates accommodation—an attitude that prevailed in the past—not merely tolerance, and forbids hostility toward any religion. "There is an unbroken history," wrote the Court, "of official acknowledgement by all three branches of government of the role of religion in American life from at least 1789." The concept of a "wall" of separation between church and state is, therefore, "a useful metaphor" but "is not a wholly accurate description of the practical aspects of the relationship that in fact exists." (104 S. Ct. 1355, 1359 [1984].) This brings to the forefront the role of the church in meeting the challenges of the twenty-first century.

In his lecture "The Church's Legal Challenges in the Twenty-First Century," Professor John Witte,

Jr., discusses both the challenges that the law of the
state poses to the ministry of the church and the
challenges the ministry of the church poses to the
law of the state. Professor Witte points out that the
era in which the church could expect special legal
protection is waning—new strategies will have to be
found to protect the church's rights and liberties.
As for the influence of the church on the society at
large, Professor Witte expects that this will largely
be in the area of human rights—emphasizing the
responsibilities that are entailed with such rights
along with the God-given dignity of every individual.

Professor Witte examines the heritage of the
three great Christian traditions—Catholic, Protestant, and Orthodox—in promoting human rights to
determine how the church may best serve as their
advocate in the future. Each tradition is founded on
theological ideals basic to human rights (such as
conscience, dignity, and love) and has developed its
own system to promulgate these ideals. He points
out that the whole system of human rights legislation that has grown up throughout the world in the
last half century has its roots in Christian theology.

The history of the modern world reveals the
necessity for such legislation. The deep-seated and
intolerable discontent of the underprivileged classes
has frequently brought about turmoil and even revolution, but such revolution has produced only tragic
misery. The totalitarian regimes produced by such

revolutions have led to the condemnation of pity, of compassion, of self-sacrifice, and of faith in the dignity and worth of every individual.

Education has a significant role in providing the type of leadership that will prevent such catastrophes as the French and Bolshevik revolutions, which caused so much suffering and the loss of the lives of so many millions of people. Such leadership is not founded on birth, wealth, or party membership but on experience, intellectual capacity, and— most of all—dedication to one's fellowman. This kind of leadership is needed to reduce, if not eliminate, the vast extremes between wealth and poverty and the decline of the middle class, both of which threaten the fabric of our society.

In the business world, economic efficiency is indispensable to the success of enterprise, but such success cannot endure when the businessperson's activities violate the rights of his fellowman to self-respect, a decent standard of living, and dignity. In the long run, what is morally wrong can never be economically fruitful, and no economic action can be sound unless it fits into an accepted system of values. Expediency does not preclude the entrepreneur's concern for the welfare of his fellowman. It was Dr. Samuel Johnson who said that "a decent provision for the poor is a true test of civilization."

Accepting social responsibility is not only an ethical precept but also the wisdom and law of life. In order to succeed economically, the business-person has to channel his efforts, talents, energies, and intelligence into avenues that will lead his business to prosper. His efforts, however, must be combined with his leadership in promoting the well-being of the society in which he lives. Such responsibility does not undermine the springs of free initiative—the cornerstone of business endeavor in a free society.

Professor Joanne B. Ciulla in her lecture "Business Leadership and Moral Imagination in the Twenty-First Century" observes that the moral standards that apply to business will not change in the new century which is approaching. But the increasing complexity of the problems that those in business will face will require new understanding in order to meet these challenges. The world of business is becoming increasingly decentralized, both because of new technology and because of changing social structures. Leaders will find that it will be necessary to use persuasion and imagination to achieve their goals, rather than rely on the authority of their positions.

One positive result of recent technological changes, Professor Ciulla points out, is that it has become increasingly difficult to hide misconduct or poor business decisions. The private lives of leaders have become increasingly public and thus increasingly important. Furthermore, workers are becoming increasingly sophisticated and suspicious of promises of shared power that only increase their work load and yield no real influence in corporate decisions.

Many of the most complex challenges awaiting us in the coming century concern the technologies of medicine. The heated discussion in Congress about the future of Medicare and Medicaid relates to only one of the issues raised in the field of health care. Bitter disputes cover many other issues such as abortion, which has become a subject of controversy in determining the scope of the platforms of our competing political parties; medical malpractice law, the abuses of which have reached the magnitude of a serious threat to the free exercise of health care by hospitals, physicians, pharmacies, and nurses; the ethical and religious aspects of surrogate motherhood and of genetic engineering; and the extent of care that should be offered to the mentally retarded, to the severely senile, or to those affected by Alzheimer's disease. In the heat of these disputes, abortion clinics are bombed and physicians performing abortions are killed. The controversies concerning the definition of death, assistance to accelerate the death of the hopelessly ill, and the determination of when a fetus is viable and the question of its use for medical purposes to alleviate the suffering caused by illness have gained not only medical and moral but also political significance.

There exists a distinction between secular and religious bioethics. The bioethics that has become a household word is a secular discipline that has developed in the last two or three decades. It is concerned with health care ethics as well as questions about the moral values raised by health care.

The word *moral* derives from the Latin word *mores*, and *ethics* from the Greek word *ethos*; both source-words refer to traditional human behavior. The word *ethics*, however, is most often used in reference to professional conduct. A professional code of ethics is the consensus of expert opinion as to a necessary standard within a profession. Morality deals with right human conduct in a more general context.

Like truth, morality belongs to a group of terms that includes such values as religion, justice, beauty, and conscience, all of which have a great impact on human life. Without going deeper in analyzing the differences between ethics and morality, we can say for the purpose of our discussion that both terms call for a reverence for life, defined by Albert Schweitzer when he wrote:

"Let me give you a definition of ethics: It is good to maintain life and further life; it is bad to damage and destroy life. . . . Ethics is the maintaining of life at the highest point of development—my own life and other life—by devoting myself to it in help and love, and both these things are connected." (*Reverence for Life*, Philosophical Library, New York, 1965, pp. 34-35.)

We may say that the roots of Schweitzer's thought can be found in the fundamental tenet of the prophecies of Amos, Hosea, Jeremiah, and Isaiah and in the preaching of Jesus and of Paul the Apostle.

In his lecture "Beyond the Harm Principle: From Autonomy to Civic Responsibility," Bruce Jennings puts biomedical issues into a wide context. Mr. Jennings realizes that these issues involve the fundamental tension between freedom and responsibility—and points out that the pendulum currently has swung drastically in the direction of emphasizing personal autonomy in almost every situation. He examines the principles on which such ideas of autonomy are philosophically based and finds them inadequate as foundations for social behavior or for moral understanding.

Mr. Jennings illustrates his argument with an examination of one area of bioethics that has changed radically in recent years: smoking and the use of tobacco. Never in history, he points out, have public attitudes changed so drastically in such a short time. Formerly, it was assumed that an individual's right to smoke was part and parcel of his autonomy; no arguments that he was hurting himself were strong enough to allow governmental interference. It was only when some research results suggested that passive smoke inhalation might contribute to cancer that the tide shifted. Mr. Jennings argues that the whole debate should have been on different ground—that there are important values other than autonomy that our society does not, but should, take into account.

In conclusion, let me say that the readers of this volume of proceedings will find that in the 1995 Lectures on Moral Values in a Free Society the theme is repeatedly stressed that man was meant to be free and that the responsibility for the welfare of the nation and of the individual can be discharged without depriving the people of their right to exercise their freedom as long as dangerous self-centeredness is not causing its abuse. Our liberties should not be so construed as to excuse acts of licentiousness or to justify practices—divorced from ethical principles—inconsistent with peace, good order, and the prosperity of our communities.

The lecturers also stress man's freedom of choice—a choice between a life based on moral values and one separated from such values. They express hope that the dominant force in the twenty-first century will be a morality with roots in compassion and generosity that will pervade the fabric of our national life. Only such a morality can satisfy the spiritual needs of all mankind.

MORAL VALUES OR THE WILL
TO POWER

by

Andrew R. Cecil

Andrew R. Cecil

Andrew R. Cecil is Distinguished Scholar in Residence at The University of Texas at Dallas. The University established in his honor the Andrew R. Cecil Lectures on Moral Values in a Free Society in February 1979 and invited Dr. Cecil to deliver the first series of lectures in November of that year. The first annual proceedings were published as Dr. Cecil's book The Third Way: Enlightened Capitalism and the Search for a New Social Order, *which received an enthusiastic response. He has also lectured in each subsequent series. A new book,* The Foundations of a Free Society, *was published in 1983.* Three Sources of National Strength *appeared in 1986, and* Equality, Tolerance, and Loyalty *in 1990. In 1976 the University named for Dr. Cecil the Andrew R. Cecil Auditorium, and in 1990 it established the Andrew R. Cecil Endowed Chair in Applied Ethics.*

Educated in Europe and well launched on a career as a professor and practitioner in the fields of law and economics, Dr. Cecil resumed his academic career after World War II in Lima, Peru, at the University of San Marcos. After 1949, he was associated with the Methodist church-affiliated colleges and universities in the United States until he joined The Southwestern Legal Foundation in 1958. Dr. Cecil helped guide the development of the Foundation's five educational centers that offer nationally and internationally recognized programs in advanced continuing education. Since his retirement as President of the Foundation, he serves as Chancellor Emeritus and Honorary Trustee.

Dr. Cecil is author of fifteen books on the subjects of law, economics, and religion and of more than seventy articles on these subjects and on the philosophy of religion published in periodicals and anthologies. A member of the American Society of International Law, of the American Branch of the International Law Association, and of the American Judicature Society, Dr. Cecil has served on numerous commissions for the Methodist Church and is a member of the Board of Trustees of the National Methodist Foundation for Christian Higher Education. In 1981 he was named an Honorary Rotarian.

MORAL VALUES OR THE WILL TO POWER

by

Andrew R. Cecil

The French expression *fin de siècle* has much stronger connotations and conveys a more powerful image than the English phrase "end of the century." The French words conjure up decadent elements that pervaded the atmosphere at the end of the nineteenth century. The English phrase, on the other hand, looks forward rather than backward. Implicit in its reference to the end of an age is the new century just entering the new horizon.

The light in which the approaching new century is seen now, at the end of the twentieth century, varies from unprecedented pessimism projecting a literal end of the world to unbridled optimism that foresees daily travel to the moon and cities built in outer space. Given the momentum of scientific as well as economic progress, it seems safe to foresee new achievements in medicine and technology as well as continued expansion of business activity in the years that lie ahead.

The Ultimate Virtues

But in trying to look ahead to the changes a new century will bring, one overwhelming question, transcending mere technical or economic development, remains: Will morality, with its roots in compassion and generosity, be the dominant force in governing human relationships? Or will the new century extol power for its own sake and—in a world divorced from ethical principles—exalt hypocrisy, fraud, and force as the normal patterns for life?

A. The "Moral Sense"

To the British philosopher Anthony Ashley Cooper, the third Earl of Shaftesbury (1671-1713), is attributed the term "moral sense," referring to man's natural sense of right and wrong in a universe which is essentially harmonious. Shaftesbury saw no conflict between man's natural impulses toward happiness and well-being and the need for attention to the welfare of society as a whole. Along with the term "moral sense," Shaftesbury also expressed a belief in "knowledge of right and wrong" and in "reason in moral judgment." His main contribution was the term "moral sense," but he did not make important advances in developing a true theory of an innate moral sense.

It was Francis Hutcheson (1694-1746), a professor of moral philosophy at the University of Glasgow, who developed the moral sense theory in more detail. Hutcheson's moral sense theory maintained that because of his social nature, man possesses an "inborn sense" that permits him to discern moral values and attitudes. In his "benevolent theory" of moral conduct, Hutcheson argued that men can have a disinterested motive in acting for the sake of the benefit of others without seeking their own advantage. The moral sense is the feeling of approval a man gets from his fellowman when his actions are guided by the motive of benevolence. The satisfaction from virtuous and benevolent behavior arises not from the benefits it brings to the one who practiced it but from the beauty and merits of the act itself.

B. *The Categorical Imperative*

The idea of a moral sense that is innate and not derived from experience was adopted by the philosophers known as the intuitionists. Foremost among them was the German metaphysician Immanuel Kant (1724-1804). Kant's belief in an innate moral sense came out of the British philosophical tradition epitomized by Shaftesbury and Hutcheson, whose ideas he called "a beautiful discovery of our age." However, Kant wanted to move from the vague apprehension of an internal moral sentiment to something more rational. Foremost among his philosophical ideas was the demonstration of a rational basis for moral behavior.

Kant found this basis by accepting in his metaphysical system a universal moral law as pragmatically necessary. He described this universal moral law as the supreme *a priori* principle of morals. This supreme principle of morals is truly *a priori* because it does not depend on experience past, present, or to come. It is as absolute and certain as mathematics. Such a pure moral law inexorably binds every man as the "categorical imperative": the unconditional command of one's conscience to "act as if the maxim of your action were to become through your will a Universal Law of Nations."

What this statement means is that the principle by which an individual acts "manifests itself as an unconditional demand that has no need to borrow its validity from some further end, but instead possesses its own validity in that it presents an ultimate, self-evident value." (Ernst Cassirer, *Kant's Life and Thought*, trans. by James Haden, Yale University Press, 1981, p. 245.)

The demands the categorical imperative imposes Kant calls "duty." The only thing that sets man apart from the animals, Kant believed, is this sense of duty. Men act in obedience to such an inner sense of duty, which is free from questionable self-experience. It shows what man's obligations are and compels him to fulfill those obligations. The inner sense of duty demanded by the categorical imperative forms the basic, autonomous concepts of morality and contrasts sharply with the emphasis on rights and personal liberty unimpeded by any concern for others that has become so characteristic of the end of the twentieth century.

Kant admitted that every day we learn that expediency is not the justification for virtue. We are reminded of Glaucon and Thrasymachus, the Sophists portrayed in the first book of Plato's *Republic*, who argue that "all men believe in their hearts that injustice is far more profitable to the individual than justice." (*The Republic and Other Works*, trans. by Benjamin Jowett, Anchor Books, 1973, p. 48.) For them, the shrewdness and slyness of the serpent turn out to be more profitable than the innocence and meekness of the dove. But while Plato's two Sophists insist that "the just is always a loser in comparison with the unjust" (*Id.*, p. 27) and that injustice applied on a large scale is particularly rewarding, since "injustice, when on a sufficient scale, has more strength and freedom and mastery than justice" (*Id.*, p. 28), Kant believed that all men, when faced with injustice, still feel in their hearts the command of righteousness.

We should note that the Roman statesman and philosopher Cicero believed that

"there never can be such a thing as a conflict between expediency and moral rectitude. . . .

[No] greater curse has ever assailed human life than the doctrine of those who have separated [the two concepts of morality and expediency]." (*De Officiis*, trans. by Walter Miller, Harvard University Press, 1961, pp. 277, 301.)

In my previous Lectures on Moral Values in a Free Society, I have tried to make a distinction between expediency in the short and long runs. The apparent benefits of immoral expediency are short-lived, as evidenced by many historical events that have taken place in this century. Adolf Hitler enjoyed military victories at the beginning of World War II, Joseph Stalin expanded the Soviet empire, and the followers of apartheid claimed political gains and economic prosperity. In the long run, however, what is morally wrong cannot be expedient, as demonstrated by the defeat of Germany, the collapse of the Berlin Wall and communism, and the end of apartheid.

For Kant, the demands of expediency make no claim on human actions. This life is only a prelude to a life of enlightenment where the just will receive their reward. This leads to the postulate of immortality and to the postulate of the existence of God found in *The Critique of Practical Reason*: "I will that there be God, that my existence in this world be also an existence in a pure world of the understanding outside the system of natural connections, and finally that my duration be endless."

(*The Critique of Practical Reason and Other Writings in Moral Philosophy*, trans. by Lewis White Beck, The University of Chicago Press, 1949, p. 245.)

Morality stands independent in Kant's philosophy, which rejects theology as a basis of morals. For Kant, religion is based on morals, and theology makes only a supplementary contribution. (Our courts have described the relationship between morality and religion as follows: "For what is religion, but morality with a sanction drawn from a future state of rewards and punishment?" *McAllister v. Marshall*, 6 Bin. 338, 6 Am. Sec. 458 PA [1814].)

Kant's religious beliefs were greatly influenced by his pietistic parents. Pietism, an anticlerical movement in the Lutheran church popular between the latter part of the seventeenth and the middle of the eighteenth centuries, insisted on the moral responsibility of the individual and on a strictness of religious practice. Its practices included serious Bible study, devotional meetings to bring Christians into inspiring fellowship, preaching aimed at the spiritual needs of men, and direct contact with God. Pietism put "religion of the heart," good works, quiet faith, and living according to Bible rules above ritual and dogmas.

C. The Spirit of the Gospel

Influenced by Pietism, Kant believed that religion disappears where statutes, creeds, symbols, or ceremonies replace the devotion to universal moral law. "Christ," he wrote, "has brought the Kingdom of God nearer to earth; but he has been misunderstood: and in place of God's Kingdom, the kingdom of the priest has been established among us." (H.S. Chamberlain, *Immanuel Kant*, Vol. I, Gordon Press, 1972, p. 570.)

Kant makes a distinction between the clergyman as a representative of the church who is obligated to preach sermons about conforming to the symbols of the church he serves (for he has been accepted on this condition) and the clergyman as a scholar:

"But as a scholar he has complete freedom, even the calling, to communicate to the public all his carefully tested and well-meaning thoughts on that which is erroneous in the symbol and to make suggestions for the better organization of the religious body and church. In doing this, there is nothing that could be laid as burden on his conscience." (*What Is Enlightenment?* in Beck, p. 288.)

Kant's motto concerning enlightenment is "Have courage to use your own reason." (*Sapere aude.*) Enlightenment is "man's release from self-incurred tutelage, [which is] man's inability to make use of his understanding without direction from another." A man's point of enlightenment is his escape from the dictates of the dogmas of others, chiefly in matters of religion. (*Id.*, pp. 286, 291.)

In order "to bring the Kingdom of God nearer to earth," Kant believes, the dignity and worth of every individual should be respected. Kant maintains that it is a crime against the dignity that belongs to every man "to use him as a mere means for some external purpose." He condemns colonialism and its barbaric and inhuman behavior in treating the aboriginal inhabitants "as nothing" and domination over them as "equivalent to a conquest." (*Eternal Peace and Other Essays*, Boston, 1914, p. 68.)

Kant stresses equality of opportunity for every individual so that he can apply his talents and abilities in pursuing his personal development and happiness. We can find ideas similar to Kant's incorporated in our Constitution and Bill of Rights, which reject hereditary privileges and prerogatives of birth and class.

Whether the principles of morality are described by Shaftesbury as a "moral sense," formulated by Kant as the "categorical imperative," or simply announced by the spirit of the Gospel, they offer a challenge to the forthcoming century. This challenge is whether to adopt and follow these principles or to turn to another kind of "morality"—a philosophy of power that sees strength as the ultimate virtue.

Prophets of Destruction

Our forefathers found the moral as well as political foundations of our society "self-evident." The truths they acknowledged were grounded not only in the rich heritage of the Judaeo-Christian tradition but also in the philosophical tradition (epitomized, as we have seen, by Kant) that believed a moral compass is to be found deep in the hearts and consciences of all men.

Another philosophical tradition—a deeply pernicious one—has grown increasingly influential over the last century and a half. It can be seen most clearly in the writings of the German philosopher Friedrich Nietzsche (1844-1900). Instead of morality, Nietzsche extols power. Nietzsche condemns the old Judaeo-Christian morality of compassion and self-sacrifice, of the dignity and equality of every individual. In Nietzsche's scheme of things, poverty is not a "proof of virtue." Equality brings "decadence and descending life." Sympathy and pity are a waste of feeling for the incompetent and helpless.

A. The Gospel of the Superman

Nietzsche argues that the traditional morality proclaimed in the philosophical and religious traditions should be replaced by his new basic conception: "The world is the will to power—and nothing besides!" In *Thus Spoke Zarathustra*, he reveals his own ideal of human conduct by proclaiming the gospel of the Superman (*Ubermensch*)—a higher form of mankind that he envisioned as the next step on the evolutionary ladder. Because of his aristocratic superiority, the Superman represents the aim and meaning of life. In a world of danger and duplicity, only the Superman, by his own superiority, will survive. He represents an aristocratic existence that excludes the common herd.

The philosophies and religions that Nietzsche considers decadent stress the virtue of peace. For Nietzsche, the very aspiration to a state of power is victory. He wrote:

"The great confusion on the part of psychologists consisted in not distinguishing between these two kinds of pleasure—that of falling asleep and that of victory. The exhausted want rest, relaxation, peace, calm—the happiness of the nihilistic religions and philosophies; the rich and living want victory, opponents overcome, the overflow of the feeling of power across wider domains than hitherto." (*The Will to Power*, trans. by Walter

Kaufmann and R.J. Hollingdale, Vintage Books, 1968, p. 374.)

Resistance and obstacles incite the will to power: "[T]his game of resistance and victory arouses most strongly that general feeling of superabundant, excessive power that constitutes the essence of pleasure." (*Id.*, p. 371.)

In *The Anti-Christ*, Nietzsche defines what is good and what is bad:

> "What is good?—All that heightens the feeling of power, the will to power, power itself in man.
>
> "What is bad?—All that is born of weakness.
>
> "What is happiness?—The feeling that power *increases*,—that a resistance is overcome.
>
> "Not contentment but more power; *not* peace at all, but war; not virtue but proficiency (virtue in the Renaissance style, *virtu*, virtue free of moralic acid)." (*The Anti-Christ*, in *Twilight of the Idols and The Anti-Christ*, trans. by R.J. Hollingdale, Penguin Books, 1968, pp. 2-3.)

Nietzsche abhors moralities that say, "Do not do this! Overcome yourself!" To follow such moralities obsessed with the negative, he believes, leads to impoverishment. He rejects "negative" virtues, "virtues whose very essence is to negate and deny oneself something." (*The Gay Science*, in *Works*, Vol. 2, Munich, 1955, p. 180.) Dangers have a positive value and merit respect:

> "The nations which were worth something, which *became* worth something, never became so under liberal institutions: it was a *great danger* that made of them something deserving reverence, danger which first teaches us to know our resources, our virtues, our shield and spear, our *spirit*,—and which *compels* us to be strong." (*Twilight of the Idols*, p. 93.)

The courage of self-exposure to danger means strength to Nietzsche.

The value Nietzsche places on superabundant, excessive power; strength; war; and the overcoming of resistance leads the German philosopher to contempt for the Judaeo-Christian ethic, since it demands service and self-sacrifice. Christianity, he maintains, belongs to the *Heerden-moral* (the morality of the herd), which should be distinguished from the *Herren-moral* (the morality of the superior master).

In Nietzsche's view, Christianity's demand for justice, humility, brotherhood, and responsibility for our fellowman breeds the morality of slaves.

The slavish masses, in their humility and helplessness, idealize weakness. Jesus, with his code of kindness and gentleness, is the epitome of such weakness. Strength, aggressiveness, and cruelty are to Him totally foreign. Nietzsche idealizes masters rather than slaves—masters who would combine courage, manhood, and a strong will that would lead toward superiority and the creation of the Superman. The road of the Superman leads to the destruction of Christianity.

One of the features of the Superman is his complete lack of conscience. Conscience, Nietzsche believes, is a Jewish, Christian, and democratic concept, reducible to a love of easy security and a system of rewards for the meek, the poor, and the sick—all of whom Nietzsche despises. (His desire to breed the Superman was a direct foreshadowing of Nazi insistence on racial purity, genetic experimentation, and euthanasia of the unfit.)

The "spiritual men" of Christianity, he argues, have given comfort to the sufferers, courage to the oppressed and despairing; by preserving the sick and the suffering, they have caused the European race to deteriorate. "I regard Christianity," he writes, "as the most fatal and seductive lie that ever yet existed—as the greatest and most injurious lie. . . . I urge people to declare open war with it."

Nietzsche realizes that his philosophical stance is diametrically opposed to that of Kant. He writes:

"Kant's success is merely a theologian's success. . . . A virtue merely from a feeling of respect for the concept 'virtue,' as Kant desired it, is harmful. . . . Nothing works more profound ruin than any 'impersonal' duty, any sacrifice to the Moloch of abstraction. Kant's categorical imperative should have been felt as *mortally dangerous!* . . . Kant became an idiot." (*The Anti-Christ*, pp. 121-122.)

Nietzsche deeply resented Kant's status as the leading German philosopher and did all in his power to undercut it.

As Nietzsche himself predicted, his ideas have had a profound effect on the real world. The philosopher has proved a prophet of the destruction that followed in the wake of his philosophy. He eagerly looked forward to the ruin of Christian morality and called it "the great spectacle of a hundred acts that will occupy Europe for the next two centuries, the most terrible and problematical but also the most hopeful of spectacles." (*The Genealogy of Morals*, in *The Birth of Tragedy and The Genealogy of Morals*, trans. by Francis Golffing, Doubleday Anchor Books, 1956, pp. 297-98.) It may be noted that Hitler and Stalin did declare war against religion and revived cruelty in a form never known before. Terrible indeed was the spectacle they brought about—but only in the absence of all humane values could anyone find such a spectacle "hopeful."

B. The Absolute Power of the Ruler

Judging by the joy some people derive from bullfights, crucifixions, public executions, and other tragedies, Nietzsche concludes that "man is the cruelest animal" and that cruelty has constituted his great joy and delight since ancient times. This kind of cruelty, the philosopher observes, is the effect of a desire for power—but he is far from condemning such a desire. In fact, it forms the basis of his thinking.

For Nietzsche, the will to life finds its expression not in the "miserable struggle for existence" but in a "Will to War, a Will to Power, a Will to Overpower." He sees evil in the poor, meek, and weak who fail and good in the mighty, strong, and rich who survive and win. For Nietzsche, life is will to power and, therefore, it is essentially "injury, conquest of the strange and weak, suppression, severity . . . and at least, putting it mildest, exploitation." Exploitation, he believes, is a primary organic function of living; "it is a consequence of the intrinsic Will to Power, which is precisely Will of Life."

Nietzsche was not the first prominent philosopher to claim that, in the public arena, might makes right and that the end can justify the most savage means. Almost four hundred years before his time, the Florentine statesman, historian, and political writer, Niccolò de Bernardo Machiavelli (1469-1527), also advocated the use of cruelty; a ruler "must not mind incurring the charge of cruelty for the purpose of keeping the subjects united and faithful." (*The Prince*, The New Library, 1952, p. 89.)

Although Machiavelli does not preach the gospel of the Superman, he exalts the absolute power of the prince. He divorces a ruler from ethical principles, recommending that he use hypocrisy, force, and fraud to gain power. Nothing, according to Machiavelli, causes a prince to be so much esteemed as giving proof of prowess. Since it is difficult for a ruler to be both loved and feared, "it is much safer for a ruler to be feared than loved." (*Id.*, p. 90.) He should not hesitate "to act against faith, against charity, against humanity, and against religion" in order "to maintain the state." (*Id.*, p. 93.)

By divorcing the study of effective politics from the study of ethics, Machiavelli completely severs himself from the traditional concepts of the power that conscience should wield over individuals. In his writings, which became the blueprint for the efforts of generations of dictators and absolute monarchs, he stresses that the root of political expediency is force, unrestricted by considerations of generally accepted moral values.

In order to achieve political ends, Machiavelli argues, a ruler may lie, deceive, intrigue, conspire, or use any kind of crooked means. In foreign policy, "a prince should therefore have no other aims or thought, nor take up any other thing for his study, but war and its organization and discipline, for that is the only art necessary to one who commands." (*Id.*, pp. 46-47.)

The desire for power combined with a dismissal of conscience is expressed effectively by the title character in Shakespeare's *Richard III*:

"Our strong arms be our conscience, swords our law.
March on, join bravely, let to 't pell-mell;
If not to heaven, then hand in hand to hell."

Shakespeare's villains, in fact, often speak doctrines derived from the teaching of Machiavelli, who was regarded as an infamous atheistic writer in Elizabethan England.

It seems that *Thus Spoke Zarathustra* and *The Prince* continued to serve as handbooks for such dictators as Mussolini, Hitler, and Stalin and his successors, who in accordance with maxims prescribed by Nietzsche and Machiavelli sought, through tyranny, increased power offering injustice and slavery instead of justice, equality in general poverty instead of prosperity, imperialism instead of peace, and hypocritical slogans to conceal the darkness of oppression.

In our generation, we have witnessed the fall of fascism in Italy, the fall of Nazi Germany, the fall of communism in Soviet Russia and in the satellites, and the fall of apartheid in South Africa. These old, threatening ideologies are, however, not dead. From all over Europe, we see on the nightly news or on the front pages of our newspapers pictures of Nazi "skinheads" with their straight-arm salutes and their uniforms "ornamented" with swastikas—haunting reminders of an era of terror, cruelty, and oppression. These street hooligans continue to terrorize foreigners, vandalize Jewish cemeteries, and burn down refugee shelters. In France, the ultrarightist party, the National Front; in Britain, the British National Party; and in Italy, the National Alliance are seeking and gaining representation in parliamentary elections. The other, equally dangerous, end of the political spectrum also shows alarming signs of continuing life. In Russia and in other countries that lived under the communist regime, the communists are still raising their heads, disguised as socialists.

The events that followed World War II, including the defeat of fascism, nazism, and ultimately communism, give us hope in the principle that nothing established by violence and maintained by force, in opposition to what is right, can endure. Nor can anything which is based on a contempt for human personality and which degrades humanity endure.

As we enter the twenty-first century, we should be reminded of the warning Aristotle issued in his *Politics*: "For man, when perfected, is the best of the animals, but when separated from law and justice, he is the worst of all: . . . wherefore, if he have no virtue, he is the most unholy and the most savage of animals!" What distinguishes human beings from animals is freedom of choice—a choice between a life based on moral values and a life separated from moral values. This fundamental choice can be made correctly only through a profound understanding of the purpose of life.

The Widening Gap Between the Rich and the Poor

The twentieth century has been marked by formidable events that have changed the course of history and the map of the world—to mention only two World Wars; the end of colonialism and the birth of many new sovereign nations; the collapse of fascism and nazism and the largely broken back of communism (with remnants in China, North Korea, and Cuba); and the postwar recoveries of Europe and the defeated nations of Germany and Japan. The end of this century, however, leaves us with great challenges to be faced in the new millennium. One of the maladies of the *fin de siècle* is the vast and growing gap between the rich and the poor and the decline of the middle class.

In his 1994 commencement address at Harvard University, Vice President Al Gore quoted a survey indicating that in 1965 the percentage of those questioned that believed that government favors the rich and the powerful was 29 percent. By 1994 it had grown to 80 percent. ("Cynicism or Faith: The Future of a Democratic Society," *Vital Speeches of the Day*, Vol. LX, No. 21, Aug. 15, 1994, p. 646.) According to *Time* magazine, a new study says that the United States has the largest gap of any major industrial country. ("Who Is Really to Blame?" November 6, 1995, p. 36.)

In describing the success of the United States in becoming the world's most competitive economy, *Time* magazine's cover story of October 24, 1994, "We're #1 and It Hurts," also points out the high cost of this success: wave after wave of downsizing layoffs, wage increases limited or forgone, and replacement of full-time workers by part-time or temporary hired hands. Our economy seems to display two faces; we are developing a two-tiered society. Corporate profits (and executive salaries) keep rising rapidly while real wages (discounted for their purchasing power) are static. Those officially defined in 1994 as poor, with an annual income of $15,141 or less for a family of four, constituted 14.5 percent of the U.S. population in 1994.

A twelve-member panel of experts at the National Academy of Science that convened in 1992 upon the recommendation of Congress suggested significant changes in the official definition of poverty. The poverty measure used by the federal government for three decades was based on family size and its cash income before taxes. The panel's proposal suggests basing the definition of poverty on disposable income. Such income would include not only cash income but also noncash government benefits such as subsidized housing, food stamps, school lunches, and home energy assistance. Under the proposal, the family cash income would be reduced by taxes, child care costs, work expenses, out-of-pocket medical expenses, and child support paid from the payer's income. The recommended changes, if approved by Congress (although unlikely to be embraced by the Republican majority), could substantially increase the number of American families classified as poor.

Over the last three decades, the growth of the gross national product was not accompanied by a decrease in poverty. In 1964 Congress passed Medicare, one of the many programs President Lyndon Johnson in his War on Poverty promised would "eliminate poverty from the land." Yet in 1994 a higher percentage of the population lived in poverty than when President Johnson left office in 1969. American real wages—adjusted for inflation—have fallen 7 percent in twenty years; blue-collar wages have fallen 8 percent in only seven years.

The Economic Policy Institute, using the figures compiled by the Bureau of Labor Statistics, concludes that the median family income declined $3,110 between 1989 and 1993 when adjusted for inflation. This decline of the median family income—made worse because the value of antipoverty programs such as food stamps and Aid to Families with Dependent Children (AFDC) was decreasing with inflation—caused the welfare roles to swell.

Pope John Paul II has been stressing in his encyclicals that "savage" capitalism may not in its consequences be an improvement on Marxism. The untamed engine of greed, camouflaged as the economic self-interest required by capitalism, has brought about a rash of mergers, buyouts, and hostile takeovers, which have been followed by the layoff of thousands of workers. Companies enjoying record profits continue to lay off employees. AT&T, for instance, has eliminated 140,000 jobs since 1984. Recently a merger between Chase Manhattan and Chemical Bank was announced. The resulting company is expected to cut 12,000 jobs.

While hundreds of concerns are gobbled up, the underclass of unskilled workers keeps growing, increasingly isolated from existing and future workplaces. Some economists blame growing inequality on immigration and on trade with low-wage nations that depresses the wages of low-skill American workers. In fact, the biggest devaluation of American workers' skills has come from the technological revolution. The forces of growing technology and the computer have also contributed to the erosion of the middle class, some of whose members have been penalized for lacking the required skills. Wall Street is bullish on businesses that carry out programs of layoffs labeled as "reconstruction" or "reorganization." While the value of a company's shares goes up in the expectation of larger profits, those who still hold jobs are fearful for their and their children's futures.

President Truman, while serving as senator, in a speech delivered on the floor of the Senate in December 1937 sharply denounced the Wall Street "billionaires" for their greed and for not making a real contribution to national progress:

"It is a pity that Wall Street with its ability to control all the wealth of the nation and to hire the best brains of the country has not produced some statesmen, some men who could see the dangers of bigness and of the concentration of the control of wealth. Instead of working to meet the situation, they are still employing the best law brains to serve greed and selfish interest." (Merle Miller, *Plain Speaking*, Berkley Publishing Corporation, 1974, p. 146.)

The forces unleashed by mergers, "reconstruction," and new technology have brought into the labor market thousands of jobseekers with few marketable skills and little or no income. A new underclass of the disadvantaged, of the "working homeless," has become a nationwide trend in our social and economic condition. According to a report in *The Wall Street Journal* (usually considered a publication friendly to business management), persons who work full time and still cannot cover the necessities of proper food or afford to own or rent a place to live have become "a significant slice of the American work force." ("Boomtowns Lure Poor With Plenty of Work—But Not Much Else," *The Wall Street Journal*, June 16, 1994, p. A1.)

Technology and globalization have resulted in more economic and geographical segregation by wealth. According to a study published by the Twentieth Century Fund, the wealth of the richest 1 percent of U.S. households climbed from 20 percent of all stocks, bonds, savings accounts, home equity, and other private assets in the mid-1970s to 35.7 percent in 1989. Furthermore, in 1969 the top 20 percent of American households received 7.5 times the income of the bottom 20 percent. (Edward N. Wolff, *Top Heavy: A Study of the Increasing Inequality of Wealth in America*, The Twentieth Century Fund Press, 1995, pp. 62-63.) In 1992 the richer households had 11 times the income of the poor—compared to the ratio of 7 to 1 in Canada and Great Britain and of 5.5 to 1 in Germany in 1992. (*Newsweek*, May 1, 1995, p. 62D.) A large factor in the growing gap between the rich and the poor is that most of the growth in jobs over the last decade in the United States has been in the services sector—and such jobs frequently pay far less than the manufacturing jobs in heavy industry, which have traditionally been the bastions of organized labor. Many new jobs in such fields as restaurants (especially fast food restaurants) pay only minimum wage or a little more.

The *Wall Street Journal* article chronicles the plight of such workers in the "boomtown" of Branson, Missouri, which has become a popular tourist destination as a mecca for fans of country music. Don Mullins, a plumber from Austin, Texas, moved to Branson in 1993 with his wife, two unemployed sons, and their wives and children. They could not afford the security deposits or utility down payments that would have been necessary to rent an apartment, so all eleven family members continued to sleep in a 28-foot trailer for most of a year. At the time the story was written, members of the family held down five jobs. They had five children and about five square feet per person. The newborn baby slept in the sink.

Other full-time workers in Branson found it necessary to seek even less satisfactory accommodations. Nancy and John Rogers and their four sons

were living in a homeless shelter by the railroad
tracks and eating their dinners in the shelter's soup
kitchen. Mr. Rogers was working as a security
guard on the night shift for minimum wage, and
Mrs. Rogers had a job at a local poultry plant.
Those who were worse off—newcomers to town
looking for jobs—were sleeping in dumpsters, in
their cars, or under bridges. ("Boomtowns," *The
Wall Street Journal*.)

Senator Hubert H. Humphrey once observed
that "the true moral test of government is how it
treats those in the dawn of life—the children; those
who are in the twilight of life—the aged; and those
who are in the shadow of life—the sick, the needy,
the handicapped."

Are we taking care of the aged, the sick, the
needy, and the handicapped? According to a study
conducted by the Urban Institute (a private, non-
profit social and economic policy-centered group
based in Washington), as many as 4.9 million elderly people—about 16 percent of the population aged
sixty and over—are either hungry or malnourished
because they are poor or too infirm to shop or
cook. The Administration of Aging office reports
that "the hunger and malnutrition of older persons
are becoming more serious and severe" and that
senior centers across the country are facing length-
ening waiting lists for federal meals programs.

Not only elderly people suffer from hunger.
According to a report issued by the privately funded

National Center for Children in Poverty, 6 million, or 26 percent of children under six, are living in poverty. We are spending billions of dollars to remove farm land from production while our children go hungry.

The Struggle for Equality and a Decent Standard of Living

In the last three decades of the twentieth century, we have witnessed a rise in the proportion of two-earner families. During the last decade, the rise has been in the proportion of three-job marriages. Six percent of the American workforce occupies 15 million jobs. When women entered the labor force in huge numbers, it was expected that dual job-holding would provide enough additional income to meet family needs. The rise of three-job marriages proves that extra income is still needed to pay the bills.

Female employment has continued to climb and has been accompanied by a rise in the average age at which women marry, a rise in the divorce rate, and a decline in family size. The increased participation of women in the labor force has spurred a great deal of concern about the strength of the traditional family in our society and the care we give our children. The issue of child care has thus gained a prominent place on the national agenda.

The struggle for a decent standard of living and for equality will continue. This brings up a question: At what kind of equality are we aiming?

The famous watchwords of the French Revolution, "Liberté, égalité, fraternité," became the rallying cry of many subsequent generations of reformers the world over. Among these three ideals of liberty, equality, and brotherhood, the goal of equality has the most complex ramifications in mankind's quest to implement it. It can lift the weak up to the level of the strong, or it can drag the strong down to the level of the weak. The second alternative has repeatedly ignited bloody revolutions that have brought about confusion, stress, and terror and, when they missed their mark, have given birth to emperors and totalitarian dictators.

The first alternative, lifting the weak to the level of the strong, represents the distinctive American concept of equality focused on giving each citizen an opportunity to make his own place in society. It does not demand equality of wealth or confiscation of property and its division among the poor and homeless. Abraham Lincoln advised, "Let not him who is houseless pull down the house of another, but let him work diligently and build one for himself, thus by example assuring that his home should be safe from violence when built."

Bigness may be fascinating, but it may also be frightening—especially when a society is being pulled apart between an overclass of those earning

more than the average American family and the
crumbling underclass, largely trapped in inner cities
besieged by crime and squalor. Among the phenomena reflecting this increased inequality is the growing number of multimillionaires and billionaires.
Management experts, union leaders, and rank-and-
file employees will continue to wonder why the
chief business executives of our corporations are
earning several times the salaries of their often
more successful Japanese competitors. Extreme
practices of executive compensation in which remuneration reaches the figure of tens if not hundreds
of millions of dollars has become a question of
moral integrity. Theodore P. Houser, a former
chairman of Sears, Roebuck and Company, pointed
out:

> "The services of great educators, great scien-
> tists, great public servants are equally invalu-
> able to the country. Such services are not put
> exclusively or even primarily on a cash basis.
> If we sincerely believe that the publicly-owned
> American corporation is the most efficient and
> most desirable means of serving the material
> and, to some extent, the cultural needs of the
> people, then those endowed with the ability to
> lead these great organizations should begin to
> conceive of their remuneration partly in terms
> of the satisfaction of making a real contribution
> to national progress." (*Big Business and Human*

Values, McGraw Hill Book Company, Inc., 1957, pp. 27-28.)

On a similar note, former President of Harvard University Derek Bok wrote: "Under the glare of publicity and scholarly analysis, performance pay for top executives has turned out to be a sham and an embarrassment that has undermined the public's confidence in business leadership." (*The Cost of Talent*, The Free Press, 1993, p. 111.)

Suggestions about how to address this moral issue have been made and will continue to be made. They include limiting top salaries to amounts no more than twenty-five times a company's lowest-paid employees, prohibiting salaries larger than that of the President of the United States, correlating salaries with a company's performance over several years rather than merely with annual profits, and requiring stockholder approval of executive contracts.

In discussing the various remedies to curb excessive compensation of business executives, Bok concludes: "In the end, therefore, no remedy yet proposed promises to cure all the ailments that afflict executive compensation. Granted, the worst abuses may mercifully come to an end." (*Id.*, p. 117.) Excessive remuneration is basically more a moral and social than an economic issue. Poverty breeds strife and envy, which is more irreconcilable than hatred. Confucius once wrote, "It is harder to be poor without murmuring than to be rich without arrogance."

There is an undercurrent of hostility on the part of the poor and hungry toward those who possess and enjoy an extravagant abundance. But while the lavish raises in executive salaries will remain an object of concern and criticism, curbing salaries will not heal the split of society into the rich and the poor. Even if business executives begin to conceive of their remuneration partly in terms of making a contribution to the prosperity of their country, this alone will not "lift the weak to the level of the strong" and will not provide food and shelter for homeless unskilled job seekers or for the "working homeless."

The Decline of the Middle Class

The widening gap between the rich, who are getting richer, and the poor, who are getting poorer, is not conducive to social cohesion. Because the distance between the two poles—the growing underclass increasingly isolated from sources of income and wealth and the small overclass increasingly gathering more and more of society's wealth and income—is widening, we must seek remedies to counterattack this vastly increased inequality and to reverse the decline of the middle class.

This split in American society cannot be remedied by graduated tax rates or by the expansion of our degrading welfare system. Secretary of Labor Robert Reich wrote in a column for *The New York Times* that he sees the foundation for improvement in proper training and education. (Robert B. Reich, "The Fracturing of the Middle Class," *The New York Times*, August 31, 1994, p. A19.) Numerous studies confirm that the labor force divides workers by education and skills. In 1992 a male college graduate earned 83 percent more than a man with only a high school diploma. Between 1979 and 1989, college-educated women increased their earnings 16 percent, while earnings of women with high school educations or less remained about the same. The inflation-adjusted earning of men with no education past high school fell 14 percent. Unemployment among high school dropouts was more than 12 percent in 1992, while for workers with college degrees it amounted to only 3 percent. Computers have made striking changes in the business world, but only one in ten high school dropouts uses computers at work, while two-thirds of college graduates do.

The Commerce Department's *Statistical Abstract of the United States* reports that some 63 percent of all American high school graduates receive some form of higher education. According to studies conducted by business magazines and regional Federal Reserve banks, less than 5 percent of students from the low-income quadrant complete college, versus about 75 percent in the best-off quadrant of families. In colleges, a remarkable shift to explicitly vocational curricula is taking place among undergraduates. Between 1971 and 1988, the percentage of students earning baccalaureate degrees in engineering, business, and other professional programs rose from 30 to 50 percent. (Aaron Bernstein, "Inequality: How the Gap Between Rich and Poor Hurts the Economy," *Business Week*, August 15, 1994, p. 78.)

At great economic cost, we are making efforts to open the doors of the academy to all. Each year millions of those who desire education beyond high school are taking out educational loans that may be repaid as a percentage of future income. Under President Bill Clinton's administration, 20,000 young people who enter national service will earn money that they can apply to a college education. Technical jobs going to those with four-year college degrees or associate's degrees from community colleges will form the core of employment for the new middle class of the technically trained.

The Role of Institutions of Higher Learning

The importance of the middle class cannot be overemphasized. Already in ancient Greece, Aristotle recognized the role of a large middle class in providing cities with a good government, saying that it "has a great steadying influence and checks the opposing extremes" of the rich and the poor. If, however, the creation of a middle class is focused on those acquiring technical skills through universal access to colleges and universities, a question arises whether the sole purpose of education is to make money. Does our commitment to building the foundations of a new middle class of technicians debase the ideals of education, including education for citizenship? Should our universities and colleges become factories turning out skilled professionals without regard to the traditional aims of liberal education?

Our institutions of higher learning have the responsibility to shape the ideals and habits of well-informed citizens. As Spinoza expressed it, "Men are not born for citizenship, but must be made for it." The mind of John Stuart Mill, whose essay *On Liberty* epitomized nineteenth-century British ideas of liberalism, was shaped in just this way. He was taught Greek at the age of three and read Plato at the age of eight, when he also began to study Latin. When he was about thirteen years old, he took a course on political economy, during which he read Adam Smith and David Ricardo. At fourteen he was studying French language and literature. His concern for the nature and limits of power that can be legitimately exercised by society over the individual can in large measure be attributed to his education.

The splendid fruit of Mill's nurturing education does not imply that all children are gifted with his brilliance and could benefit from such training at so early an age. It may, however, justify the conclusion that mankind would have been deprived of his writing, with its worldwide impact, if his education, like that of so many of our contemporaries, had been limited to technology or computer science.

We may justly expect that our educational institutions train future leaders responsive to the hopes and aspirations of the people, who in a democracy ultimately shape the nation's destiny. We may justly expect that educational institutions will discharge their responsibility to prepare well-educated citizens for participation in our democracy by exposing students to the knowledge of the past and to the moral questions arising in human relations. Writing about the Peloponnesian War in the fourth century B.C., Thucydides stressed the importance of "knowledge of the past as an aide to the interpretation of the future, which in the course of human things must resemble if it does not reflect it." Since ancient times, exposure to moral values shaping human relations has given educated citizens the ability to cope with the problems confronting every society, such as the preservation of freedom and justice and the continued search for stability and public order.

Socrates taught that a rightly trained mind would naturally turn toward virtue. The "right" training calls not only for intellectual development but also for imparting spiritual insight that illuminates ways of discharging our responsibility toward our country and toward world society.

Education is not limited to the process of communicating a given skill to successive generations. Alongside intellectual discipline, it has to fulfill the purpose of building character upon the foundation of moral principles. A concern for virtue and spiritual values is the very core of the existence of academic institutions, whether public, private, or church-related.

All men are born to equal political and civil rights, but this does not mean that all men are born with equal powers and faculties. The damages caused by destructive ideas of egalitarianism, or "political correctness," are extremely high: Students of great ability are deprived of opportunities to develop their talents; academic curricula are diluted with proliferating nonintellectual courses; entrance and graduation requirements are weakened or abolished and grades inflated; authority at school and at home collapses; and the moral standards that safeguarded society against cultural degeneration and sterility are rejected.

The concentrated efforts of our institutions of higher learning on such subjects as mathematics, foreign languages, history, philosophy, culture, and a reverence for our heritage will not create an elitism paving the way toward a class of intellectual aristocracy. The American tradition of equality rejects the concept of society as an organization of unequal classes with different rights and duties. Intellectual excellence does not conflict with our belief that every kind of labor is an honorable calling. Those acquiring the skills to become technicians and computer analysts or operators, for instance, become valuable members of the middle class.

The American idea of equality stresses the unalienable birthright of everyone in all areas of life. In stressing intellectual development we are also stressing the purpose of equality in freedom—a freedom that gives each person the opportunity to rise as high as merit will carry him. All people, regardless of their educations, are born to equal political and civil rights. This ideal of personal equality in freedom remains the fundamental tenet of our nation's political faith. Preserving the integrity of our institutions of higher learning does not conflict with, but rather undergirds, this political faith by stressing the virtues of citizenship as well as the duties of citizenship that must be discharged with absolute loyalty to the public interest.

Conclusion

The creation of a new middle class is an urgently needed but a slow process. Unfortunately, the gap between the rich and poor is growing at a much faster rate. According to an October 1995 report of the U.S. Census Bureau, more than 38 million

Americans (about 14.5 percent of the American people) lived in poverty in 1994. This includes close to 15 million children who are still living in poverty. (However, if Medicare, Medicaid, and other government-funded benefits were counted as income, the poverty rate would fall to 12.1 percent.)

In 1992, if a family of four earned $27,380 it was considered low-income. Nearly 42 percent of American children grow up in low-income families, and about 23 percent—almost one child in four—grow up in poverty. More than half of the food stamps program serves to feed children. (One in ten Americans now receives food stamps.)

According to the 1994 Census Bureau report published in October 1995, the top 5 percent of Americans in 1994 earned 21.2 percent of the total national income. The bottom 20 percent earned 3.6 percent. In 1989, the top 5 percent accounted for 18.9 percent of all income, while the lowest 20 percent garnered 3.8 percent. The growth of our economy since 1989 has generated more income, but it was obviously channeled to those in the top 5 percent. This economic growth has not been solving the problems of poverty and the disturbingly unequal distribution of income in our society.

This unequal distribution of wealth and income and the gap between the powerful rich and the oppressed and weak poor was of concern to the writers of the Old and New Testaments and to many subsequent religious leaders and philosophers throughout the centuries. In the Old Testament, prophetic judgment is leveled against those "which oppress the poor, which crush the needy" (Amos 4:1) and those who "swallow up the needy, even to make the poor of the land to fail" (Amos 8:4). Jesus' blessing upon the poor and His pronouncement of woe upon the rich, as recorded in Luke's version of the Beatitudes, maintain the same concern for the weak and the oppressed.

In the fourth century, St. Ambrose, bishop of Milan and Doctor of the Church, preached:

"Thou then, who has received the gift of God, thinkest thou that thou committest no injustice by keeping to thyself alone what would be the means of life to many? It is the bread of the hungry that thou keepest, it is the clothing of the naked that thou lockest up; the money that thou buriest is the redemption of the wretched."

In our own century, Karl Barth, the Swiss theologian (1896-1968), wrote:

"The Church is witness of the fact that the Son of man came to seek and to save the lost. And this implies that—casting all false impartiality aside—the Church must concentrate first on the lower and lowest levels of human society. The poor, the socially and economically weak and threatened, will always be the object of its primary and particular concern, and it will always insist on the State's special responsibility for these weaker members of society." (*Community, State and Church*, Peter Smith Press, 1968, p. 173.)

This spirit of the Gospel and the voices of St. Ambrose and Karl Barth are the voices of the "moral sense," of Kant's "categorical imperative" described earlier. In disregarding this voice, we may face the danger of tragedy that occurs when despair turns into anger. The French and Bolshevik Revolutions were caused by the deep-seated, intolerable discontent of the underprivileged classes. These two revolutions also gave vivid illustrations of what happens when the fortunes of events transmute the weakness of the poor and the oppressed into strength and a desire for power. This "will to power" led to the condemnation of pity, of compassion and self-sacrifice, and of faith in the dignity and worth of every individual. Like Nietzsche's Superman, the revolutionaries abhorred morality. Like Nietzsche, they placed all value in power, strength, aggression and cruelty.

The purpose of education for citizenship is to provide the type of leadership that will prevent such catastrophes as the French and Bolshevik Revolutions, which caused suffering, misery, and the loss of the lives of millions of people. This type of leadership is not founded on birth, wealth, or party membership. Thomas Jefferson pointed out, "There is a natural aristocracy among men. The grounds of this are virtue and talents." This natural "aristocracy," which Jefferson believed to be "the most precious gift of nature," calls not for egalitarianism but for vesting the responsibility for our destiny in the hands of educated men and women who excel in intellectual capacity, in experience, and—most of all—in dedication to their fellowman.

INDIVIDUALISM BEFORE MULTICULTURALISM

by

Glenn C. Loury

Glenn C. Loury

Glenn C. Loury is University Professor and Professor of Economics at Boston University. He previously taught economics and public policy at Harvard University, Northwestern University, and the University of Michigan. He holds a B.A. in Mathematics from Northwestern and a Ph.D. in Economics from M.I.T. Dr. Loury has published many scholarly articles in the fields of microeconomic theory, industrial organization, natural resource economics, and the economics of income distribution. He has been an advisor and consultant with state and federal government agencies and private business organizations in his fields of expertise.

Dr. Loury has given lectures on his research before numerous scholarly meetings and academic societies in North America and Europe. He has been a visiting scholar at Oxford University, Tel Aviv University, the University of Stockholm, and the Institute for Advanced Study in Princeton. He has been the recipient of a Guggenheim Fellowship to support his work and has served as an economist on several advisory commissions for the National Academy of Sciences.

In addition to his work as an economic theorist, Dr. Loury has been widely involved in public debate and analysis of the problems of racial inequality and social policy toward the poor in the United States. His essays and commentaries on these topics have been featured in the New York Times, Wall Street Journal, The Public Interest, Commentary, The New Republic, *and many other publications. He has often been asked to offer his views on national television and has made public speaking appearances around the country. Dr. Loury's critical analyses of issues such as affirmative action, social welfare, and civil rights policies have been noticed and discussed by opinion leaders in business, politics, and the legal community. A collection of his writings on politics and culture was published by The Free Press in early 1995 under the title* One by One, From the Inside Out: Essays and Reviews on Race and Responsibility in America.

INDIVIDUALISM BEFORE MULTICULTURALISM

by

Glenn C. Loury

Since the Founding, America has struggled to incorporate the descendants of African slaves into an estate of full and equal citizenship. One hundred thirty-two years after the Emancipation Proclamation, this process, though well advanced, remains incomplete, and we must now consider whether, and how, further progress can be made. But we must first decide who "we" are.

Who *we* are depends on who's talking and to whom. In our society, public race-talk is part of the larger political conversation concerning national affairs. But there is private race-talk too—that conversation among segregated confidants who speak with a candor not possible in public. Civil rights, affirmative action, multicultural education, and voting rights policy are discussed publicly in explicitly racial terms while the implicit racial themes of crime and welfare simmer beneath the surface of public conversation. Race-talk has always dominated communal deliberations among blacks as we have sought, through heated internal dialogue, to come to terms with the inherited disability of second-class citizenship. I am sure that whites, too, engage in lively, if guarded, private deliberations on race-related matters.

These two levels of deliberation—public within the national polity and private amongst blacks and whites ourselves—interact in important and complex ways. What is acceptable and effective to argue in either forum depends on the nature of the discourse in the other. Prudent discussion of racial matters must attend to these interrelated contexts. So, I am engaged here in two connected but distinct conversations, practicing a kind of "double speak," if you will. On the one hand, I speak as a public man, an American, to the whole nation, offering advice on how "we"—that is, all of us—should approach questions of race. But, as a black I will be seen (by whites and blacks) to be addressing "my people" about how "we" should endeavor to make progress. This dual role limits what I can say without risk of misunderstanding by one or another audience. Both audiences may extend to me a certain license because of race but, for the same reason, may also demand a certain fealty: Each listener will search for evidence of disloyalty to cherished values and for confirmation of strongly held convictions. Inevitably, some of you must be disappointed.

As a veteran of the academic culture-wars during a period of growing racial conflict in our society, I have often had to confront the problem of balancing my desire to fulfill the expectations of others—both whites and blacks, but more especially blacks—with my conviction that one should live with integrity. Sometimes this has led me to act against my initial inclination in ways which would elicit approval from my racial peers. After many years, however, I came to understand that unless I were willing to risk the derision of the crowd, I would have no chance to discover the most important truths about myself or about life, to define and pursue that which I most value, or to make the unique contribution to my family and community which God has endowed me to do. (The stakes are now too high for any of us to do otherwise.)

This small private truth points toward some larger social truths—that the seductive call of the tribe can be a siren's call; that there are no group goals or purposes existing prior to, and independently of, the life plans and the ideals of individual persons; that unless individualism is truly exalted, multiculturalism descends into crass ethnic cheerleading; that, after all is said and done, race is an epiphenomenon, even here in America, even for the descendants of slaves.

Race-talk like this is heresy for those I call racialists. Racialists hold to the doctrine that "authentic" blacks must view themselves as objects of mistreatment by whites and share in a collective consciousness of that mistreatment with other blacks. For decades, believers of this creed have shaped the broad public discussion of racial affairs in America; they have also policed, and therefore stifled, black communal discourse. They have argued, in effect, that the fellow feeling amongst blacks engendered by our common experience of racism should serve as the basis for our personal identities. Only if whites fully acknowledge their racist culpability, they insist, can the black condition improve. In this they have been monumentally, tragically wrong. They have sacrificed, on an altar of racial protest, the unlimited potential of countless black lives. And they are not alone. Whites who view blacks first as representatives of a group, and only secondly as individuals, are racialists too. Whether the patronizing liberal or the contemptuous conservative, the effect of such white racial essentialism is to diminish the humanity of blacks.

The ineluctable truth of the matter is that the most important challenges and opportunities confronting any person arise not from his racial condition, but from our common human condition. Group membership alone tells us nothing that is true about how we should live. The social contingencies of race, gender, class, or sexual orientation are the raw materials from which an individual constructs a life. The life project is what brings about the development and expression of an individual's personality. Whatever our race, class, or ethnicity, we must all devise and fulfill a life plan. By facing and solving this problem, we grow as human beings and give meaning and substance to our lives.

Because we share this problem—identical in essentials, different only in details—we can transcend racial difference, gain a genuine mutual understanding of our respective experiences and travails, and empathize with one another. As Sartre might have said, because we all confront the existential challenge of discovering how to live in "good faith," we are able to share love across the tribal boundaries.

From the Inside Out

Ironically, to the extent that we individual blacks see ourselves primarily through a racial lens, we sacrifice several possibilities for the kind of personal development that would ultimately further our collective racial interests. For if we continue to labor under a self-definition derived from the outlook of our putative oppressor, confined to the contingent facts of our oppression, we shall never be truly free men and women.

The greatest literature of ethnic writers begins from this truth. In *A Portrait of the Artist as a Young Man*, James Joyce says of Irish nationalism: "When the soul of a man is born in this country there are nets flung at it to hold it back from flight. You talk to me of nationality, language, religion. I shall try to fly by these nets. . . . Do you know what Ireland is? . . . Ireland is the old sow that eats her farrow." Just as Irish nationalism stultified Stephen Daedalus in *A Portrait*, so too has the racialist emphasis on a mythic, authentic blackness worked to hold back the souls of young blacks from flight into the open skies of American society.

At the end of chapter 16 of *Invisible Man*, Ralph Ellison's hero recalls a lecture on Joyce that he heard while in college at Tuskegee, Alabama, in which the teacher argues:

"(Joyce's) problem, like ours, was not actually one of creating the uncreated conscience of his race, but of creating the uncreated features of his face. Our task is that of making ourselves individuals. . . . We create the race by creating ourselves and then to our great astonishment we will have created a culture. Why waste time creating a conscience for something which doesn't exist? For you see, blood and skin do not think!" Further on in this passage the hero concludes: "For the first time, lying there in the dark, I could glimpse the possibility of being more than a member of a race. It was no dream, the possibility existed. I had only to work and learn and survive in order to go to the top." (Vintage Books, 1972, pp. 345-46.)

This is precisely the point. Ellison understood it. A later generation of black writers have refused to see it: Skin and blood do not think. The "conscience of the race" must be constructed from the inside out, one person at a time. If this is a social truth, it has important consequences for political life and discourse in contemporary America.

My colleague Charles Griswold has nicely captured the impossibility of discourse in a society that is dominated by mutually insulated groups—those who define themselves by race, from the outside in. In a recent essay he writes:

"One frequently hears people declare, with passion: 'Speaking as an [X] I can inform you that

[Y]', where 'X' is the name of the relevant group and 'Y' stands for some description or evaluation of the condition or beliefs of X. An auditor not in group X cannot speak with any authority about that group; one must and usually does defer immediately. The moral authority embodied in statements preceded by 'Speaking as an [X]' stems in part from an epistemic thesis to the effect that the point of view shared by all members of X is not accessible, or at least not sufficiently accessible, to non-X persons." (Charles Griswold, "Adam Smith on 'Sympathy' and the Moral Sentiments," unpublished draft, Department of Philosophy, Boston University, 1994, p. 22.)

Griswold is interested in the paradox of these mutually insulated groups, neither capable of understanding the other, who nevertheless insist upon equal group recognition. This is an apt description of the current state of American pluralism. But we must ask whether recognition can reasonably be demanded when understanding is denied to the outsider. How can genuine respect arise from mutual ignorance? How can the white, who has "no idea of what black people have endured in this country," really honor the accomplishment of blacks who have transcended the barriers of racial constraint? How can a black who could "never see things the way the white man does," ever hope to persuade that "white man" to meet him halfway on a matter of mutual importance?

It would appear that empathy and persuasion across racial lines are impossible unless an understanding obtains that the conditions and feelings of particular human beings are universally shared. Such an understanding can be had, but only if we look past race to our common humanity. This implies that the problems facing poor, black Americans should not be presented as narrow racial claims, but should be conveyed to the rest of the polity in their essential human terms. (This position is also advocated by, among others, sociologist William J. Wilson in "Race-specific Policies and the Truly Disadvantaged," Chap. 5 in *The Truly Disadvantaged*, The University of Chicago Press, 1987. Note, however, that the basis for my argument here lies deeper than the instrumental political calculation that racially targeted policies are likely to be less popular than universal policies.) From this perspective, the racialist's assertion of epistemic privilege is more than a philosophic stance. In our pluralistic democracy it leads, as Griswold notes, "to the destruction of any notion of community except as the arena within which war is waged for recognition, and for the political and economic benefits which follow from recognition."

A Politics of Despair

Black-white relations are actually far worse than Charles Griswold's assessment. Contrary to conventional wisdom, the wrong turn of black leadership was not the embrace of quotas. That move is derivative from a prior, more fundamental mistake, which was the embrace of black power and the abandonment of the integrationist ideal. Racialists have waged a "war for recognition" under the banner of black victimization for the past twenty-some years. This war has now ended with a plaintive demand to be patronized. In a stunning attempt at political jujitsu, the voices of black authenticity insist that the very helplessness of their group gives evidence of whites' culpability, to which the only fit response is the recognition of black claims. This is a politics of despair. Especially since the 1994 elections, we can see that other white responses are possible. The racialist strategy has proved disastrous.

Consider the issue of affirmative action. Advocates of blacks' interests are now reduced to insisting that affirmative action is just and necessary because without the use of special criteria for selection, the numbers of blacks in various important institutions of the society would be unbearably low. This argument is rooted in desperation.

Consider the pathetic condition of the urban black poor. They are especially vulnerable politically. Democrats all, racialist black leaders of inner-city communities have cast their lot with those seeking to expand the welfare state, increase taxes, and promulgate more regulations. Blacks reliably provide one-fourth of the Democratic votes in presidential contests. Black Congressional representation is significantly dependent on districts which have been gerrymandered so as to assure that ultraliberal black candidates are elected without the inconvenience of having to persuade any whites to support them. This political dependence on the left has persisted despite the rightward political drift of the nation ongoing for the last generation, and notwithstanding the cultural conservatism of a deeply religious black American population.

There is potential for an alliance of interests between black and white religious conservatives, along the increasingly more important cultural fault line in American politics. But this has been ignored by black leaders. (For example, after the 1994 elections Jesse Jackson attacked the Christian Coalition as reminiscent of the Nazis—neither a fair, nor a smart thing to say!) Black leaders have struck an alliance with feminists, gay activists, and civil libertarians, while building few bridges to center-right political organizations. It is now obvious that a conservative political majority can be constructed in this country, and can govern, without attending to the interests of urban minority voters. It seems equally clear that such an outcome would be unhealthy for our democracy.

Poisoning Democracy

The paradigm of racial essentialism does damage beyond politics. In *The Bell Curve* (1994), Richard Herrnstein and Charles Murray stirred controversy by pointing to a large gap in the average IQ scores between blacks and whites, and suggesting that this difference is fixed partly by genetic factors. Yet these authors can claim, with cause, that they are merely responding to the zeitgeist: their analysis brew is expressed in the racial group terms previously anointed by the advocates of social equity. They can say, in effect, "Counting by race wasn't our idea, but since you've mentioned it, let's look at *all* of the numbers!"

Black racialists are hoist with their own petard by the arguments and data of *The Bell Curve*. Having insisted on the primacy of the racial lens, they must now confront the specter of an intelligence accountancy which offers a rather different explanation for the ambiguous achievements of blacks in the last generation. The question now, for blacks as well as whites, is whether given equal opportunity blacks are capable of gaining equal standing in society. It is a peculiar mind which fails, in light of American history, to fathom how poisonous a question this is for our democracy. Some conservatives seem to believe that blacks can never pass this test; some blacks apparently agree, arguing that blacks should abandon "white America," go our own way, and burn a few things down in the process. At bottom these racial essentialists share a similar perspective.

Yet, is it really such a radical thought to assert that the challenge confronting blacks today is not racial at all? Is it not primarily the human condition, rather than a racial condition, that we must *all* learn to cope with? What Paul wrote to the Corinthians many centuries ago remains true: "No temptation has seized you except what is common to man; but God is faithful, He will not allow you to be tempted beyond your ability, but when you are tempted He will provide a way out so that you can bear it." The Greek word for *temptation* here can also be translated as *trial* or *test*. If indeed blacks must now bear-up under the weight of a great human trial, still God remains faithful.

Whatever the merits and demerits of IQ tests, the scores need not be bandied about in aggregate terms of race. If low intelligence is a problem, then a change in the racial identities of those at the top and bottom of the IQ scale would not lessen the problem. Similarly, the crime problem in our society has nothing to do with the skin colors of the perpetrators and victims. Why do we talk of "black crime"? This too easily adopts a racialist perspective. Consider the construction "Jewish embezzlement." It shocks the ear, as it should; perhaps this makes it easier to see my point. It is a great—if common—moral and political error to advance the view that a person's race is his most important characteristic. For liberals to make victims of a handful of vicious criminals—who happen to be black, and who prey disproportionately upon other blacks—is an egregious act of racialist propaganda. The result is not to engender sympathy in the minds of whites, but instead to foster fear of and contempt for the communities from which these criminals have been advertised to have come. Smugly confident of their moral superiority in pursuit of "racial justice" for death row inmates, the racialists are unable to see how shrill and hysterical their claims sound to the average American.

Honor and Identity

In his 1982 study *Slavery and Social Death*, Orlando Patterson rejects a property-in-people conception of slavery. Instead, he defines slavery as the "permanent, violent domination of natally alienated and generally dishonored persons." The novelty of this definition lies in its emphasis on the systematic *dishonoring* of enslaved persons. Patterson argues that hierarchical symbolic relations of respect and standing between masters and slaves are the distinguishing features of the institution of slavery. He finds it a common feature of slavery that masters parasitically derive honor from their power over slaves, while slaves are marginalized by virtue of having no social existence except that mediated by their masters.

Patterson's insight into the nature of slavery implies that emancipation—the legal termination of the masters' property claims—cannot by itself possibly suffice to make genuinely equal citizens of slaves (or their descendants). Freedmen must also overcome a historically generated and culturally reinforced "lack of honor"—a matter that formal legal resolutions alone cannot dispel. How are the deeply entrenched presumptions of inferiority, of intellectual and moral inadequacy, to be extinguished? How are the doubts of former masters and the self-doubts of former slaves to be transcended?

This "problem of honor" is a tenacious ideological remnant of our origins as a slave society. It must be faced if we are to live up to the ideal of *E pluribus unum.* Securing the respect of whites and enhancing self-respect has been a central theme in black American history. The late historian Nathan Huggins clarified the matter by noting that blacks, unlike the various American immigrant groups, are not an *alien* population in this society, but an *alienated* one—an essentially indigenous people who by birthright are entitled to all the privileges and immunities of citizenship. The political history of black Americans may be instructively viewed as the struggle to secure an acknowledgment of this birthright claim. Our goal has always been to belong to the *unum.* Despite various separatist movements, the wisest African Americans have known that inclusion is the only way. But this pursuit of freedom and inclusion is a very hard road. Booker T. Washington understood that blacks would have to confront the "problem of honor," and its demands, in their efforts to achieve true emancipation. Washington argued:

"It is a mistake to assume that the Negro, who had been a slave for two hundred and fifty years, gained his freedom by the signing, on a certain date, of a certain paper by the President of the United States. It is a mistake to assume that one man can, in any true sense, give freedom to another. Freedom, in the larger and higher sense every man must gain for himself."

Washington also knew that progress for blacks in our democracy depended upon being sensitive to the concerns of whites. Indeed, every black leader of any influence has worked within such a context. Only in our time has the notion been advanced that "authentic" black leadership should be unencumbered by the need to consider white opinion. Only in our time, to repeat, are electoral districts drawn so that blacks may be elected without the inconvenience of winning white votes.

Persuasion or Extortion?

The old civil rights activism sought to persuade; the new activism seeks to extort. Martin Luther King, Jr., and his followers protested vigorously on behalf of clear principles of social justice. Their use of nonviolent civil disobedience drew forth the affirmation of common principles from their fellow citizens. Their reliance on the humanity and decency of the American majority showed respect for the moral integrity of their fellows. King was thus rightly a leader of both black and white Americans. His stature in each community depended upon his influence in the other. The dramatic public confrontations he and others in the movement engineered were viewed by white and black audiences—each aware that the other was watching. The morally persuasive nature of King's appeal mobilized the conscience of the white majority. By doing so, he also convinced many blacks that there was realistic hope, at long last, that their essential interests would be accommodated. King thus confronted the most critical task of any leader who seeks to promote racial harmony in our divided society: to assure the "good people" of each race that their counterparts on the other side do, in fact, exist.

That so many young blacks see in Malcolm X and Martin King a legitimate polarity of philosophic alternatives is a telling commentary on the moral confusion of today's orthodoxy. Yet Malcolm X is an exceptionally poor guide, especially concerning blacks and the American *unum*, since the interests of blacks, properly understood, are inescapably intertwined with the concerns and sensibilities of whites. But it is to the radicalism of Malcolm X that the Afrocentrist, rejectionist rabble-rousers like Al Sharpton look for inspiration. And it is precisely because the civil rights establishment has itself lost sight of the need to take whites' fears and revulsions seriously that it falls mute in the wake of the excesses of Sharpton, Jeffries, Farrakhan, et al., who, rather than persuade on the basis of a common humanity, issue demands from their racial bunkers.

We can see the consequences of this racial insularity in Crown Heights, New York. Murderous mobs of black youths rampaged, openly incited by Sharpton and others, who then claimed status and prestige for themselves as brokers of the peace. Leaders like Sharpton have emerged because more respectable black advocates have abandoned that cardinal principle which Washington understood so well. The dominant message of these leaders is that blacks have abjured persuasion, hold white opinion in contempt, and seek to frighten and extort. Such "leadership" apparently intends to ensure that bad people of both races will find each other, the better to keep conflict alive.

The truth is that whites do not need to be shown how to *fear* black youths in the cities; instead, they must be taught how to *respect* them. This means that effective, persuasive black leadership must project to whites the image of a disciplined, respectable black demeanor. That such comportment is consistent with protest for redress of grievance is a great legacy of the civil rights movement. But more than disciplined protest is necessary. Discipline, orderliness, and virtue *in every aspect of life* will contribute to the goal of creating an aura of respectability and worth. Such an aura is a valuable political asset, and the natural by-product of living one's life in a dignified, civilized manner.

Because racial oppression tangibly diminishes its victims, in their own eyes and in the eyes of others, the construction of new public identities and the simultaneous promotion of self-respect are crucial tasks facing those burdened with a history of oppression. Without virtuous character and public citizenship, there can be no genuine recovery from past victimization. But thankfully, overcoming the accumulated disadvantages of past victimization is not an experience unique to black Americans. It's *not* just "a black thing, which you wouldn't understand."

A prominent civil rights leader teaches young blacks the exhortation: "I *am* somebody." True enough, but the crucial question then becomes: "Just *who* are you?" The black youngster should be prepared to respond: "Because I *am* somebody I will not accept unequal rights. Because I *am* somebody, I will waste no opportunity to better myself. Because I *am* somebody, I will respect my body by not polluting it with drugs or promiscuous sex. Because I *am* somebody—in my home, in my community, in my nation—I will comport myself responsibly, I will be accountable, I will be available to serve others as well as myself." It is the doing of these fine things, not the saying of any fine words, which proves that here *is* somebody to be reckoned with. A youngster *is* somebody not because of the color of his skin, but because of the content of his character.

Toward the Unum

How can we begin to overcome the fragmentation of the *unum* that is the result of racialist politics? I propose that we suppress as much as possible the explicit use of racial categories in the conduct of public affairs. This will, of course, not erase ethnic identity as an important factor in the society, but a conscious effort to achieve a humanistic, universal public policy and rhetoric would redound to the social, political, and psychological benefit of the minority poor in America. Racialists, of course, will dispute this. Stubborn economic inequality between groups, they will argue, gives the lie to the ideal of *E pluribus unum*. But why should we care about group inequality, *per se*? Why not focus on inequality among individual persons, and leave it at that?

The preoccupation with group inequality is usually defended on the grounds that group disparities reveal the oppression of individuals based on their group identity. This rationale is ultimately unconvincing. The Chinese in Southeast Asia, the Indians in East Africa, and the Jews in Western Europe are groups which, though subjected to oppression, have economically surpassed their oppressors. (See, e.g., Thomas Sowell, *The Economics and Politics of Race: An International Perspective*, William Morrow and Co., 1983. Sowell chronicles numerous instances around the world in which group differences in economic status do not correspond to the presence or absence of oppression.) The lesson of history is not that—absent oppression—all relevant social aggregates must reap roughly equal economic rewards. Indeed, that view ignores the economic relevance of historically determined and culturally reinforced beliefs, values, interests, and attitudes that define ethnic groups. "Historically specific cultures," political theorist Michael Walzer has observed, "necessarily produce historically specific patterns of interest and work."

Nor can we claim that the very existence of distinct beliefs, values, and interests among groups proves oppression. In effect, this is to argue that, but for historical oppression, all groups would be the same along every dimension associated with economic success. Yet, if group differences in beliefs, values, and interests bearing on economic achievement are the fruit of oppression, then so are those differences in group styles celebrated by the cultural pluralists. To put the matter simply by way of concrete example: If poor academic performance among black students reflects "oppression," then does not outstanding athletic or artistic performance spring from the same source? No. Obviously, the existence of group disparities is not a moral problem *ipso facto*. In any case, to the extent that inequality *is* a problem, it can be dealt with adequately without invoking group categories. American society has for thirty years pursued government, corporate, and academic policies as if the necessity of using racial categories were a Jeffersonian selfevident truth. The great costs to our sense of national unity arising from this fallacious course are now becoming evident.

Martin Luther King, Jr., is justly famous for his evocation of national unity in his 1963 speech "I Have a Dream," in which he said: "I have a dream that my four little children will one day live in a nation where they will not be judged by the color of their skin, but by the content of their character." Today, it is mainly conservatives who recall King's dream. And to evoke, with any passion, King's "color-blind" ideal is, in some quarters, to show a limited commitment to racial justice. In the face of formal equality of opportunity, liberals cling to race-conscious public action as the only remedy to the persistence of racial inequality. How deeply ironic that a vigorous defense of the color-blind ideal is regarded by the liberal mind as an attack on blacks. Lest this appear an exaggeration, consider the following: In her 1984 book *A New American*

Dilemma (Yale University Press), political scientist
Jennifer Hochschild argues that the unwillingness of
American courts and legislatures to override popular, democratically expressed opposition to massive,
cross-district busing for school desegregation expos-
es our nation's limited commitment to the ideal of
equal opportunity. In his 1993 bestseller *Race Matters* (Beacon Press), noted black scholar Cornel
West asserts: "Visible Jewish resistance to affirmative action and government spending on social
programs (are) assaults on black livelihood." In a
similar spirit, black Congressman Charles Rangel
(D-NY) made headlines during the 1994 campaign
when he alleged that Republicans' advocacy of tax
cuts was racist in motivation.

I submit, to the contrary, that establishing the
color-blind principle is the *only* way to secure last-
ing civic equality for the descendants of slaves. The
recent drift of some conservative discussion of
racial issues makes it all the more urgent that this
point be understood.

Dangers of Conservative Racialism

To illustrate my argument, let me briefly discuss
the recent book on race by conservative journalist
Dinesh D'Souza, *The End of Racism: Principles for
a Multiracial Society*. (For a more extended discussion see my review, "The End of Relativism," in
The Weekly Standard, September 25, 1995, pp.
46-49.) Because my problems with Mr. D'Souza's
book closely parallel my growing discomfort with

the larger discussion among conservatives of questions related to race in American society, a concise statement of these concerns may be helpful.

First, I will say what is *not* objectionable. Mr. D'Souza, who is not black, has every right to discuss openly and in unvarnished terms what he calls "the pathologies of black culture." To suggest otherwise would be to preclude a person like me from discussing, let's say, "the pathologies of white politics." Nor is it a problem for me that Mr. D'Souza sets out to refute widely held historical interpretations, arguing that American slavery bore no necessary connection to race, and that segregation was intended to protect blacks by keeping them out of the reach of hostile whites. I may not agree with him on these points, but they are fair game.

The fatal flaw I see in this book, and by extension in much conservative argument, is that it advances what, by my earlier definition of the term, is a "racialist" vision for America. As such, it is more likely to delay than to hasten "the end of racism." Mr. D'Souza would, of course, deny this. He defines racism as belief in the biological inferiority of one group relative to another, and explicitly (if weakly) argues against such a view in his book. But a *biological* definition, focused on beliefs about inherent human capacities, is less compelling in the American context than a *political* definition, focused on beliefs about who belongs to the national community of concern.

A racialist is one who says "too many of *those people* have low IQs, high illegitimacy rates, or high crime rates," rather than saying "too many of *our people*" suffer these conditions. He is one who advises blacks about "what *you people* must do," rather than speaking of "what *we Americans* must do." He sees blacks as *the Other*, aliens, apart from and a threat to American civilization, rather than as inseparably interwoven constituents of the larger social fabric. Nobody who has spent more than half an hour with *The End of Racism* can fail to see that Mr. D'Souza is, in this sense, a racialist. And he is not alone.

Conservatives talk incessantly nowadays about "black crime," "black illegitimacy," "black school failure," "black social pathology." But what has race to do with these problems, *per se*? Is there a difference in the average IQ, or the illegitimacy rate, between those living within a 100-mile radius of Knoxville and a 100-mile radius of Boston? Probably. But even the most well-informed social analysts would be hard pressed to say just what the difference is, because we do not conduct our public affairs in those terms. Nothing in the conservative governing philosophy requires race to be an essential category of social analysis, and much militates against this.

As I have discussed, liberals racialized our politics by arguing that "black suffering" required race-based remedies. Afrocentrists took a further step by projecting this divisive outlook back into history. These racialist efforts by the Left were wrong in principle, as well as in fact. They not only asserted erroneous conclusions (regarding the causes

of "black suffering" or the African origins of Western thought); they framed the discourse in improper
(that is, racial) terms from the start. It is a serious
mistake for conservatives, determined to refute the
liberals' factual claims, to maintain and reinforce
the Left's mistaken racialist outlook.

But this is precisely what Mr. D'Souza does. He
declares victory over the Afrocentrists by noting
that their search for a black Shakespeare has ended
in failure. But he misses the larger point: Such a
search was unnecessary all along, because Shakespeare belongs every bit as much to the ghetto-
dwelling black youngster as he does to the offspring
of middle-class whites. He upbraids cultural relativ-
ists for placing "other cultures . . . on the same
plane as the West" and for thinking that "minority
groups are entitled to a presumption of moral and
intellectual equality with whites." But he misses the
deeper truth: America's great problem is *moral,* not
cultural, relativism; we are too reluctant to enforce
the common Western standards that are embraced by
blacks and whites alike.

Transcending Racialism

The key principle in the area of race relations,
for liberals and conservatives alike, should be the
color-blind ideal. The challenge to be color-blind
should be deeper and more thorough-going than a
mere restraint on government actions. Liberals
should uphold this ideal when discussing the alloca-
tion of benefits—in education, employment, or

government contracting—as the conservative criticism of affirmative action emphasizes, to be sure. But, in the interest of fostering a wholesome, non-racialist conception of the national community of concern, the color-blind ideal should also govern how conservatives discuss the various maladies and deficiencies which plague the American people.

Can we be color-blind as we gaze upon welfare mothers, juvenile felons, and the cognitively deficient? In the face of such personal failings, we should see human beings with problems, not races of people plagued by pathology.

I do not intend to deny that cultural and historical influences exist or that they affect blacks and whites differently. But, we have a broad degree of discretion as to how we see, report upon, and think about these problems. We do not have to look upon our social and political world so unrelentingly through a racial lens. Liberals have done so, greatly to their discredit. Conservatives seem now to be in danger of making the same mistake.

The fundamental idea I want to convey here is that of *transcendence*—rising above our particularities, seeing beyond the parochial, looking more deeply perhaps than we are accustomed to do. Of course there can exist real differences, of religion and culture, which clash so fundamentally that they cannot be transcended by persons within the same society. But race in America is not, in itself such a difference. We have chosen to make it so.

Thus, the irony is that, when the senior class holds separate proms for blacks and whites, each group ends up "boogeying down" to forms of popular music which have evolved from common, American roots. The differences that really matter in America are rooted in social class, not in race. It is now a commonplace experience of middle-class black youngsters to "discover" their racial identities only after leaving home and joining others of their kind in the socially segregated college milieu. Yet, they need not wear their ethnicity quite so heavily, policing the number of white friends which it is permitted for *real* blacks to have. Nor is it necessary that we grown-ups look upon our social and political world so unrelentingly through a racial lens. That we have chosen to do so—all of us—suggests something about our hypocrisy, as we advocate but do not live by the color-blind ideal.

THE CHURCH'S LEGAL CHALLENGES IN THE TWENTY-FIRST CENTURY

by

John Witte, Jr.

John Witte, Jr.

John Witte, Jr., serves as the Jonas B. Robitscher Professor of Law and Ethics at Emory University in Atlanta. He convened the international conferences on Christianity and Democracy in 1991 and on Religious Human Rights in 1994 and has directed several projects and conferences on law and religion and legal history at Emory University, Harvard University, and the University of Chicago.

Professor Witte earned his J.D. from Harvard University in 1985. His publications include four edited books, Law, Religion and Human Rights in Global Perspective *(1995),* Christianity and Democracy in Global Context *(1993),* The Weightier Matters of the Law *(1988), and* A Christian Theory of Social Institutions *(1986), and 50 professional articles and book chapters on legal history, church-state relations, and legal philosophy. He has two other books under contract,* The Transformation of Western Law in the Lutheran Reformation *and* Law, Religion, and Family in the Law: The Protestant Part.

Professor Witte has lectured throughout the United States, Western Europe, and southern Africa. For the past three years, the Emory Law School Student Bar Association selected him as the Most Outstanding Professor. In 1994, the Alexander von Humboldt-Stiftung in Germany awarded him a Senior Fellowship, and the United Methodist Foundation for Christian Higher Education declared him to be the Most Outstanding Educator of 1994.

THE CHURCH'S LEGAL CHALLENGES IN THE TWENTY-FIRST CENTURY

by

John Witte, Jr.

The Challenges of the Next Century

Two legal challenges will face the Christian church in the twenty-first century. The law of the state will challenge the ministry of the church. The ministry of the church will challenge the law of the state.

The first challenge is the easier to discern. If present restrictive patterns continue, First Amendment law will profoundly affect the church's mission, ministry, and makeup in the next century. International laws will increasingly obstruct the church's foreign mission work. Property, taxation, and labor laws threaten to affect everything from the maintenance of church altars to the distribution of church assets. The law of clerical torts and sexual harassment will expose the church to pathos and profiteering on an unprecedented scale. The church is a legal association and actor. The golden age of its cultural superiority and superior legal protection is waning. It will take collective and concerted effort to protect the church's rights and liberties in the face of growing religious pluralism and in the shadows of a growing secular state.

While the first challenge concerns what the law of the state will do to the church, the second challenge concerns what the ministry of the church will do for law. This second challenge concerns the church not as a legal subject but as a legal prophet. It involves not the church's rights at law but its duties to law. How should the church bring its doctrinal teaching, liturgical healing, and moral suasion to bear on matters legal and political? How should the church translate its general principles of justice, mercy, and equity into specific precepts for legal living? Christ commanded the lawyers of his day to attend to the "weightier matters of the law" and commended many specific reforms of prevailing Jewish law. What should the church command and commend today—and in the next century?

Much of the response to this second legal challenge must be left to theologians, not to jurists. Much of their response must turn on the timeless commands of the holy Gospel, not the temporal demands of the secular law. As the church formulates its response, however, it might be edifying to hear—from a jurist's point of view—where the law of the state most needs the benefit of the church's witness. It might also be edifying to hear the wisdom of Carl Schmitt's famous maxim that "all the pregnant ideas and institutions of modern [law] are in essence secularized forms of theological doctrines

and structures." (*Politische Theologie*, 1916, p. 32.)
The modern church has a long and venerable tradition of legal and political prophecy at its disposal.
Our forebears have constantly translated the endur-
ing and evolving faith of the church into legal forms
and forums, both canonical and civil. There is a
great deal more in those dusty tomes and canons of
law than idle antiquaria or secular memorabilia.
These legal sources ultimately hold the theological
genetic code that has defined contemporary law for
what it is—and what it can be. There is a great deal
more in law and legal discourse than the Hollywood
production of *The Firm* or the O.J. Simpson trial
would have us believe. Law is not only the rules
and tricks of evidence, procedure, and the many
other legal subjects that we cultivate. Law is also a
living system of values and beliefs that depends, in
substantial part, upon the voice of the church and its
theologians for its contents and its efficacy.

The church's voice will need to be heard on
several volatile legal subjects in the next century—civil rights, religious rights, charity, education,
and family life prominently among them. On these
subjects, the church's traditional lore and contemporary platforms are the most refined. On these subjects, the church's voice will carry its greatest
moral suasion and legal influence. What will render
these legal subjects so volatile in the next century is
the growing legal and political crisis of the world
order. What will provide the church with the most

effective and integrated legal forum for voicing its views is the burgeoning law and culture of human rights.

The world is torn by crisis and paradox on this, the eve of the third millennium. On the one hand, the world has been witnessing a democratic metamorphosis of almost apocalyptic alacrity. The Berlin Wall has fallen. Eastern Europe is being liberated. The Soviet Empire is no more. African autocracies have crumbled. Apartheid has faded. Latin American dictators have ceded. Three dozen new democracies have been born since 1973. A sense of relief and pride must come over even the most crabbed cynic.

On the other hand, the world is torn by tumult and tragedy—by a moral Armageddon, if not a military one. Along with the birth of new democracy has come the bloody slaughter of Rwanda, Burundi, and the Sudan; the tragic genocide of the Balkans; the massive unrest of Central America, Western Africa, the Middle East, Southern Asia, the Korean Peninsula, and portions of the former Soviet bloc. Every continent now faces movements of incremental political unification versus radical balkanization, gentle religious ecumenism versus radical fundamentalism, sensible moral pluralization versus shocking moral relativism. Even in the older, more stable democracies of the West, bitter culture wars have aligned defenders of various old orders against an array of new deconstructionists. The abyss in America between city and country, ghetto and suburb, black and white, straight and gay, old and young, the monied and the maligned, the armed and their victims seems to grow constantly deeper. To bridge this abyss, to parse the paradoxes of simultaneous democratization and destruction of the world order, presents one of the most pressing moral challenges of the twenty-first century.

Church and state, religious and political officials must respond to these moral challenges in various—and mostly independent—ways. The church's classic callings to preach the Word, to administer the sacraments, and to minister to the needy must continue in the next century without necessary alliance with the state. The state's classic callings to wield the sword, to punish crime, and to protect order and peace must go on without necessary reliance on the church.

Where the respective callings of these two great institutions might profitably meet, however, is in the growing arena of human rights law. The law of human rights is hardly a modern invention; its roots grow back to the beginning of the second Christian millennium. But, in the past fifty years, the law of human rights has emerged as a primary forum for the articulation and resolution of disputes. It promises to be the main forum where the challenges of state law to the church can be most effectively parried, and where the challenges of church ministry to law can be most effectively proffered. And this is one forum where collective action of church, state, and other institutions is critical to any effective response to the world crisis.

Modern human rights norms will provide no panacea to the world crisis in the next century, but they will be a critical part of any solution. Churches will not be easy allies to engage, but the struggle for human rights cannot be won by the state alone. For human rights norms are inherently abstract ideals—universal statements of the good life and the good society. They depend upon the visions of human communities and institutions to give them content and coherence, to provide "the scale of values governing the[ir] exercise and concrete manifestation." (Jacques Maritain, *Human Rights: Comments and Interpretations*, 1949, pp. 15-16.) Religion is an ineradicable condition of human lives and communities. Religions invariably provide universal sources and "scales of values" by which many persons and communities govern themselves. Christianity and other religions must thus be seen as indispensable allies in the modern struggle for human rights. Their faith and works must be adduced to give meaning and measure to the abstract claims of human rights norms.

Law, Religion, and Human Rights
in the Postwar Period

The Christian church might well be seen as a controversial candidate for a constructive role in the regime of human rights. The Christian tradition has not spoken unequivocally about human rights, nor has it amassed an exemplary human rights record over the centuries. Its sacred texts and canons say much more about commandments and obligations than about liberties and rights. Its theologians and jurists have resisted the importation of human rights as much as they have helped in their cultivation. Its internal policy and external advocacy have helped to perpetuate bigotry, chauvinism, and violence as much as they have served to propagate equality, liberty, and fraternity. The blood of thousands is at the church's doors. The bludgeons of religious pogroms, crusades, inquisitions, and ostracisms have been used to devastating effect.

Moreover, the modern cultivation of human rights began in earnest fifty years ago when Christianity and the Enlightenment seemed incapable of delivering on their promises. In the middle of this century, there was no second coming of Christ promised by Christians, no heavenly city of reason promised by enlightened libertarians, no withering away of the state promised by enlightened socialists. Instead, there were world wars, gulags, and the Holocaust—a vile and evil fascism and irrationalism to which

Christianity and the Enlightenment seemed to have no cogent response or effective deterrent.

The modern human rights movement was thus born out of desperation in the aftermath of World War II. It was an attempt to find a world faith to fill a spiritual void. It was an attempt to harvest from the traditions of Christianity and the Enlightenment the rudimentary elements of a new faith and a new law that would unite a badly broken world order. The proud claims of Article I of the 1948 Universal Declaration of Human Rights—"That all men are born free and equal in rights and dignity [and] are endowed with reason and conscience"—expounded the primitive truths of Christianity and the Enlightenment with little basis in postwar world reality. Freedom and equality were hard to find anywhere. Reason and conscience had blatantly betrayed themselves in the previous decades.

Though desperate in origin, the human rights movement grew precociously in the decades following World War II. Indeed, after the 1950s a veritable rights revolution erupted in America, Europe, and elsewhere in the world. In America and Europe, this rights revolution yielded a powerful grassroots civil rights movement and a welter of landmark cases and statutes. In Africa and Latin America, it produced agitation, and eventually revolution, against colonial and autocratic rule. At the international level, the Universal Declaration of 1948 inspired new declarations, covenants, and conventions on more discrete rights, most notably the 1966 Covenants on Civil and Political Rights and on Social, Economic, and Cultural Rights. The United Nations established a Human Rights Committee and subcommissions to administer this growing body of human rights norms. Academies throughout the world produced a prodigious new literature urging constant reform and expansion of the human rights regime. Within a generation, human rights had become, in Jacques Maritain's famous phrase, the "new secular faith" of the postwar world order. (*Man and the State*, 1954, pp. 110-111.)

Christians participated actively as midwives in the birth of this modern rights revolution, and the special religious rights of Christianity and other faiths were at first actively pursued. Individual churches issued bold confessional statements and manifestoes on human rights shortly after World War II. Several denominations and the budding ecumenical church participated in the cultivation of human rights at the international level. The Free Church tradition played a critical role in the civil rights movement in America and beyond, as did the social gospel and Christian democratic movements in Europe and Latin America.

After expressing some initial interest, however, leaders of the rights revolution consigned religious groups and their particular religious rights to a low priority. Freedom of speech and press, parity of race and gender, and provision of work and welfare captured most of the energy and emoluments of the rights revolution. After the 1960s, academic inquiries and activist interventions into religious rights and their abuses became increasingly intermittent and isolated, inspired as much by parochial self-interest as by universal golden rules. The rights revolution seemed to be passing Christianity and other religions by.

This deprecation of the role and rights of religion was not simply the product of calculated agnosticism or callous apathy—though there was ample evidence of both. Leaders of the rights revolution were often forced, by reason of political pressure or limited resources, to address the most glaring rights abuses. Physical abuses—torture, rape, war crimes, false imprisonment, forced poverty—are easier to track and to treat than spiritual abuses, and often demand more immediate attention. In desperate circumstances, it is better to be a Good Samaritan than a good preacher, to give food and comfort before sermons and catechisms.

The relative silence of religious communities seemed to lend credence to this prioritization of effort. With some notable exceptions, Christians and other religious groups after the 1960s made only modest contributions to the theory, law, and activism of human rights. The general principles set out in their postwar manifestoes on rights were not converted to specific precepts or programs. Their general endorsement of human rights instruments was not followed by specific lobbying and litigation efforts. Whether most mainline religions were content with their own condition, or intent to turn the other cheek or look the other way in the face of religious rights abuses, their relative silence did considerable harm to the human rights revolution.

The deprecation of the special role and rights of Christianity and other religions from the mid-1960s to the mid-1980s has introduced two fallacies in the theory and law of human rights in vogue today.

First, this deprecation of religion has impoverished the general theory of human rights. On the one hand, it has cut many rights from their roots. The right to religion, Georg Jellinek wrote exactly one century ago, is "the mother of many other rights." (*Die Erklärung der Menschen- und Burgerrechte*, 1895, p. 42.) For the religious individual, the right to believe leads ineluctably to the rights to assemble, speak, worship, proselytize, educate, parent, travel, or to abstain from the same on the basis of one's beliefs. For the religious association, the right to exist invariably involves rights to corporate property, collective worship, organized charity, parochial education, freedom of press, and autonomy of governance. To ignore religious rights is to overlook the conceptual, if not historical, source of many other individual and associational rights. On the other hand, this deprecation of religious roles and rights has abstracted rights from duties. Christianity and other faiths adopt and advocate rights in order to protect religious duties. A religious individual or association has rights to exist and act not in the abstract but in order to discharge discrete religious duties. Religious rights provide the best example of this organic linkage between rights and duties. By deprecating religious rights, leaders of the rights revolution have also deprecated these organic connections, and have come to treat rights in the abstract—with no obvious limit on their exercise or their expansion.

Second, the deprecation of Christianity and other religions in a human rights regime has exaggerated the role of the state as the guarantor of human rights. The simple "state versus individual" dialectic assumed in conventional human rights theories leaves it to the state to protect rights of all sorts—first generation civil and political rights; second generation social, cultural, and economic rights; and third generation environmental and developmental rights. In reality, the state is not, and cannot be, so omnicompetent—as the recently failed experiments in socialism have shown. A plurality of voluntary associations or mediating structures stands between the state and the individual, religious institutions prominently among them. Religious institutions play a vital role in the cultivation and realization of all three generations of human rights. They create the conditions, if not the prototypes, for the realization of first generation civil and political rights. They provide a critical, and sometimes the principal, means to meet second generation rights of education, health care, child care, labor organizations, employment, and artistic opportunities, among others. They offer some of the deepest insights into norms of creation, stewardship, and servanthood that lie at the heart of third generation rights.

The challenge of the next century, therefore, will be to transform the Church from a "midwife" to a "mother" of human rights—from an agent that assists in the birth of rights norms conceived elsewhere to an association that gives birth and nurture to its own unique rights norms and practices. In the next century, the world of human rights will need the church's (pro-)creativity to continue to flourish and expand. The state will need the church's ministry to sustain the spirit of its rights law. The church will need the state's human rights law rights to protect its ministry.

The Christian Nurture of Human Rights: Catholic, Protestant, and Orthodox Traditions

The church must take two steps to transform itself from a midwife to a mother of human rights. First, given its checkered human rights record, the church must confess its past wrongs against rights. This first step the modern church has already taken many times—from the Second Vatican Council's confession of prior complicity in authoritarianism to the contemporary church's repeated confessions of prior support for apartheid, racism, sexism, social- ism, and anti-Semitism. For the church to wallow in guilt for its past rights violations is neither neces- sary nor constructive. For the church to confess past sin, however, is essential for the credibility of its rights witness.

Second, given the new prominence and urgency of rights talk today, the church must be open to a new "human rights hermeneutic"—fresh methods of interpreting its sacred texts and traditions that will recover and transplant those religious teachings and activities that are conducive to human rights. This second step the church has taken more gingerly. The Roman Catholic Church has stepped boldly in the aftermath of the Second Vatican Council to develop a refined human rights theology and advocacy. Mainline Protestant and Orthodox churches have been more cautious, tepidly endorsing the benefits of the human rights movement without developing a refined human rights theology or uniform human rights advocacy. The recent liberation of Orthodox churches in the former Soviet bloc and the recent explosion of Protestant involvement in Latin Ameri- can, African, and East European politics suggests that these traditions might soon step more boldly down the rights path.

A human rights hermeneutic allows us to see that Catholic, Protestant, and Orthodox traditions alike have had, and still have, much to offer to a human rights regime. Each tradition embraces theological norms that provide the basic building blocks of any human rights theory—conscience, dignity, reason, liberty, tolerance, love, duty, justice, mercy, righteousness, accountability, covenant, and community, among other cardinal concepts. Each tradition has developed its own internal legal system and has adjudicated the rights and duties of its members in a manner deserving of consideration—if not always emulation. Each tradition has its own advocates and prophets, ancient and modern, who have worked to achieve a closer approximation of human rights ideals for themselves and others.

Contrary to conventional wisdom, the theory and law of human rights is neither new nor secular in origin. To the contrary, human rights are, in large part, the secular fruits of classic Christian theology, which, given their current state, again need the church's nurture. A human rights hermeneutic allows us to reclaim long-obscured roles that the Christian traditions have played in the cultivation of human rights in the past. It also allows us to rename familiar theological and ecclesiastical patterns in these traditions that are conducive to the development of human rights in the future.

The following subsections take up in turn the past and potential contributions to human rights offered by the Catholic, Protestant, and Orthodox traditions. While each of these traditions builds on common biblical and patristic precedents, each offers a unique human rights perspective and practice which need to be part of the church's legal ministry in the next century.

A. The Catholic Tradition

The Roman Catholic Church is, paradoxically, the first and the last tradition within Christianity to embrace the doctrine of human rights.

At the opening of this millennium, the Catholic Church led the first great "human rights movement" of the West in the name of "freedom of the church" (*libertas ecclesiae*). During the Papal Revolution of Pope Gregory VII (1073-1085) and his successors, the Catholic clergy threw off their royal and civil oppressors and established the church as an autonomous legal and political corporation within Western Christendom. For the first time, the church successfully claimed jurisdiction over such persons as clerics, pilgrims, students, Jews, and Muslims and over such subjects as doctrine and liturgy; ecclesiastical property, polity, and patronage; marriage and family relations; education, charity, and inheritance; oral promises, oaths, and various contracts; and all manner of moral and ideological crimes. The church predicated these jurisdictional claims in part on Christ's famous delegation of the keys to St. Peter (Matthew 16:18)—a key of knowledge to discern God's word and will, and a key of power to implement and enforce that word and will by law. The church also predicated these new claims on its traditional authority over the form and function of the Christian sacraments. By the fifteenth century, the church had gathered around the seven sacraments whole systems of canon law rules that prevailed throughout the West.

The medieval canon law was based, in substantial part, on the concept of individual and corporate rights (*iura*). The canon law defined the rights of the clergy to their liturgical offices and ecclesiastical benefices, their exemptions from civil taxes and duties, and their immunities from civil prosecution and compulsory testimony. It defined the rights of ecclesiastical organizations like parishes, monasteries, charities, and guilds to form and dissolve, to accept and reject members, to establish order and discipline, to acquire, use, and alienate property. It defined the rights of religious conformists to worship, proselytize, maintain religious symbols, participate in the sacraments, travel on religious pilgrimages, and educate their children. It defined the rights of the poor, widows, and needy to seek solace, succor, and sanctuary from the church. A good deal of the rich legal latticework of medieval canon law was cast, substantively and procedurally, in the form of rights. To be sure, such rights were not unguided by duties, nor indiscriminately available to all parties. Only the Catholic faithful had full rights protection, and their rights were to be exercised with appropriate ecclesiastical and sacramental

constraints. But the basic medieval rights formula-
tions of exemptions, immunities, privileges, and
benefits, and the free exercise of religious worship,
travel, speech, and education have persisted, with
ever greater inclusivity, to this day.

It was, in part, the excesses of the sixteenth-
century Protestant Reformation that closed the door
to the Catholic Church's own secular elaboration of
this refined rights regime. The Council of Trent
(1545-1563) confirmed, with some modifications,
the internal rights structure of the canon law. But
the church left it largely to non-church bodies and
non-Catholic believers to draw out the secular implications of the medieval human rights tradition.
The Catholic Church largely tolerated Protestant and
humanist rights efforts in the later sixteenth and
seventeenth centuries, which built on biblical and
canon law foundations. The church grew increasingly intolerant, however, of the rights theories of
the Enlightenment, which built on secular theories
of individualism and rationalism. Enlightenment
teachings on liberties, rights, and separation of
church and state conflicted directly with Catholic
teachings on natural law, the common good, and
subsidiarity. The church's intolerance of such for-
mulations gave way to outright hostility after the
French Revolution, most notably in the blistering
Syllabus of Errors of 1864. Notwithstanding the
social teachings of subsequent instruments such as
Rerum Novarum (1891) and *Quadragesimo Anno*

(1934), the Catholic Church had little patience with the human rights reforms and democratic regimes of the later nineteenth and early twentieth centuries. It acquiesced instead in the authoritative regimes and policies that governed the European, Latin American, and African nations where Catholicism was strong.

The Second Vatican Council (1962-1965) and its progeny transformed the Catholic Church's attitude toward human rights and democracy. In a series of sweeping new doctrinal statements—from *Mater et Magistra* (1961) to *Centesimus Annus* (1991)—the church came to endorse the very same human rights and democratic principles that it had hotly spurned a century before. First, the church endorsed human rights and liberties—not only in the internal, canon law context but also now in a global, secular law context. Every person, the church taught, is created by God with "dignity, intelligence and free will. . . and has rights flowing directly and simultaneously from his very nature." (*Pacem in Terris*, para. 9.) Such rights include the right to life and adequate standards of living, to moral and cultural values, to religious activities, to assembly and association, to marriage and family life, and to various social, political, and economic benefits and opportunities. The church emphasized the religious rights of conscience, worship, assembly, and education, calling them the "first rights" of any civic order. The church also stressed the need to balance individual and associational rights, particularly those involving the church, family, and school. Governments everywhere were encouraged to create conditions conducive to the realization and protection of these "inviolable rights" and encouraged to root out every type of discrimination, whether social or cultural, whether based on sex, race, color, social distinction, language, or religion. Second, as a corollary, the church advocated limited constitutional government, disestablishment of religion, and the separation of church and state. The vast pluralism of religions and cultures, and the inherent dangers in state endorsement of any religion, in the church's view, rendered mandatory such democratic forms of government.

Vatican II and its progeny transformed not only the theological attitude but also the social actions of the Catholic Church respecting human rights and democracy. After Vatican II, the church was less centralized and more socially active. Local bishops and clergy were given greater autonomy and incentive to participate in local and national affairs, to bring the church's new doctrines to bear on matters political and cultural. The Catholic Church was thereby transformed from a passive accomplice in authoritarian regimes to a powerful advocate of democratic and human rights reform. The Catholic Church has been a critical force in the new wave of political democratization that has been breaking over the world since the early 1970s—both through the announcements and interventions of its papal see and curia and through the efforts of its local clergy. New democratic and human rights movements in Brazil, Chile, Central America, the Philippines, South Korea, Poland, Hungary, and elsewhere owe much of their inspiration to the teaching and activity of the Catholic Church.

The Catholic Church has thus come full circle. The Catholic Church led the first human rights movement of the West at the opening of the second millennium. It stands ready to lead the church's next human rights movement of the world at the opening of the third millennium—equipped with a refined theology and law of human rights and nearly a billion members worldwide. The Catholic Church offers a unique combination of local and global, confessional and universal human rights strategies for the next century. Within the internal forum and the canon law, the church has a distinctly Catholic human rights framework that protects especially the second generation rights of education, charity, and health care within a sacramental and sacerdotal context. Within the external forum of the world and its secular law, however, the church has a decidedly universal human rights framework that advocates especially first generation civil and political rights for all. Critics view this two-pronged human rights ministry as a self-serving attempt to advocate equality and liberty without the church, but to perpetuate patriarchy and elitism within. But this criticism has had little apparent effect. The Catholic Church's human rights ministry, if pursued with the zealotry shown by the current episcopacy, promises to have a monumental effect on law, religion, and human rights in the next century.

B. *The Protestant Tradition*

One of the ironies of the contemporary human rights movement is the relative silence of the Protestant churches. Historically, Protestant churches produced the most refined theories of human rights and worked tirelessly to effectuate legal reforms that would safeguard such rights. Today, many Protestant churches have been content simply to confirm human rights norms and condemn human rights abuses without deep corporate and theological reflection. To be sure, some leading Protestant theologians have taken up the subject in their writings and lectures. A number of Protestant groups within the church, particularly feminist and libertarian groups, have developed important new themes. But no systematic Protestant human rights theory or program has, as yet, taken the field.

The irony is that the Protestant Reformation was, in effect, the second great human rights movement of the West. Martin Luther, John Calvin, Thomas Cranmer, Menno Simmons, and other sixteenth-century reformers all began their movements with a call for freedom—freedom of the individual conscience from intrusive canon laws and clerical controls, freedom of political officials from ecclesiastical power and privilege, freedom of the local clergy from central papal rule and oppressive princely controls. As the radicality of the Reformation gave way to reconstruction, the reformers put in place a number of cardinal teachings that were (and still are) pregnant with implications for the birth of human rights in a democratic political order.

Classic Protestant theology teaches that a person is both saint and sinner. On the one hand, a person is created in the image of God and justified by faith in God. The person is called to a distinct vocation, which stands equal in dignity and sanctity to all others. He is prophet, priest, and king and responsible to exhort, minister, and rule in the community. Every person, therefore, stands equal before God and before his neighbor. Every person is vested with a natural liberty to live, to believe, to serve God and neighbor. Every person is entitled to the vernacular Scripture, to education, to work in a vocation. On the other hand, the person is sinful and prone to evil and egoism. He needs the restraint of the law to deter him from evil and to drive him to repentance. He needs the association of others to exhort, minister, and rule him with law and with love. Every person, therefore, is inherently a communal creature. Every person belongs to a family, a church, a political community.

These social institutions of family, church, and state, Protestants believe, are divine in origin and human in organization. They are created by God and governed by godly ordinances. They stand equal before God and are called to discharge distinctive godly functions in the community. The family is called to rear and nurture children, to educate and discipline them, to exemplify love and cooperation. The church is called to preach the Word, administer the sacraments, educate the young, aid the needy. The state is called to protect order, punish crime, promote community. Though divine in origin, these institutions are formed through human covenants. Such covenants confirm the divine functions, the created office, of these institutions. Such covenants also organize these offices so that they are protected from the sinful excesses of officials who occupy them. Family, church, and state are thus organized as public institutions, accessible and accountable to each other and to their members. Particularly the church is to be organized as a democratic congregational polity, with a separation of ecclesiastical powers among pastors, elders, and deacons; election of officers to limited tenures of office; and ready participation of the congregation in the life and leadership of the church.

Protestant groups in Europe and America have cast these theological doctrines into democratic forms designed to protect human rights. Protestant doctrines of the person and society were cast into democratic social forms. Since all persons stand equal before God, they must stand equal before

God's political agents in the state. Since God has vested all persons with natural liberties of life and belief, the state must ensure them of similar civil liberties. Since God has called all persons to be prophets, priests, and kings, the state must protect their freedoms to speak, to preach, and to rule in the community. Since God has created persons as social creatures, the state must promote and protect a plurality of social institutions, particularly the church and the family. Protestant doctrines of sin were cast into democratic political forms. The political office must be protected against the sinfulness of the political official. Political power, like ecclesiastical power, must be distributed among self- checking executive, legislative, and judicial branches. Officials must be elected to limited terms of office. Laws must be clearly codified, and discretion closely guarded. If officials abuse their office, they must be disobeyed; if they persist in their abuse, they must be removed, even if by force.

In the past, these Protestant teachings helped to inaugurate several of the great Western revolutions fought in the name of human rights and democracy. They were the driving ideological forces behind the revolts of the French Huguenots, Dutch Pietists, and Scottish Presbyterians against their monarchical oppressors in the later sixteenth and seventeenth centuries. They were critical weapons in the arsenal of the revolutionaries in England, America, and France. They were important sources of inspiration and instruction during the great age of democratic construction in later eighteenth and nineteenth century America and Western Europe. In this century, Protestant ideas of human rights and democracy helped to drive the constitutional reformation of France, Germany, Italy, and Iberia in the postwar period, and some of the human rights and democratic movements against colonial autocracy in Africa and fascist revival in Latin America.

These cardinal Protestant teachings and practices have much to offer to the regime of human rights in the twenty-first century. Protestant theology avoids the reductionist extremes of both libertarianism, which sacrifices the community for the individual, and socialism, which sacrifices the individual for the community. It also avoids the limitless expansion of human rights claims by grounding these norms in the creation order, divine callings, and covenant relationships. On this foundation, Protestant theology strikes unique balances between liberty and responsibility, dignity and depravity, individuality and community, politics and pluralism. To translate these theological principles into human rights practices is perhaps the greatest challenge facing the Protestant churches in the immediate future. The Protestant tradition needs to have its own Vatican II, its own comprehensive and collective assessment of its future role in the human rights drama. Of course, Protestant congregationalism militates against such collective action, as do the many ancient animosities among Protestant sects. But this is no time, and no matter, for denominational snobbery or sniping. Protestants need to sow their own distinct seeds of human rights while the field is still open. Else, there will be little to harvest, and little room to complain, in the next century.

C. The Orthodox Tradition

The Orthodox churches of the Mediterranean, Eastern Europe, and Russia ground their human rights theology less in the dignity of the person and more in the integrity of natural law and the human community. Orthodox churches believe in a natural law that is both written on the hearts of all persons, and rewritten on the pages of Scripture. This natural law prescribes a series of duties that each person owes to others and to God—not to kill, not to steal, not to bear false witness, not to swear falsely, not to serve other gods, and others. Humanity's fall into sin has rendered adherence to such moral duties imperative to the survival of the human community. God has called the state to assume principal responsibility for enforcing by law those moral duties that are essential to such survival.

According to classic Orthodox theology, human rights are simply the reciprocals of these divinely-ordained moral duties. One person's moral duties not to kill, to steal, or to bear false witness give rise to another person's rights to life, property, and dignity. A person's moral duties not to serve other gods or to swear falsely give rise to his right to serve the right God and to swear properly. For every moral duty taught by natural law there is a reciprocal moral right. Just as the state must translate moral duties into legal duties, so it must translate moral rights into legal rights.

On the strength of this ancient biblical ethic, Orthodox churches endorse a three-tiered system of rights and duties: (1) a Christian or "evangelical" system of rights and duties, based upon the natural law principles of Scripture, which are enforced by the canon law of the church; (2) a "common moral" system of rights and duties, based upon universal natural law principles accepted by rational persons in all times and places, which are enforced by moral agents within the community; and (3) a legal system of rights and duties, based upon the constitutional laws and social needs of the community, which are enforced by the positive laws of the state. The church is responsible not only to maintain the highest standards of moral right and duty among its subjects, but also to serve as a moral agent in the community, to cultivate an understanding of "common morality," and to admonish pastorally and prophetically those who violate this common morality.

Accordingly, the Orthodox episcopacy has issued numerous manifestoes on the rights of persons, based on natural law, and condemned violations of human rights, particularly in the Balkans, Eastern

Europe, and the Soviet Union. The World Congress of Orthodox Bishops (1978), for example, greeted the thirtieth anniversary of the United Nations Declaration of Rights with the call: "We urge all Orthodox Christians to mark this occasion with prayers for those whose human rights are being denied and/or violated; for those who are harassed and persecuted because of their religious beliefs, Orthodox and non-Orthodox alike, in many parts of the world." Two years later, the twenty-fifth Clergy-Laity Congress of the Greek Orthodox Archdiocese of North and South America pronounced, on the strength of "a universal natural law," that "human rights consist of those conditions of life that allow us fully to develop and use our human qualities of intelligence and conscience to their fullest extent and to satisfy our spiritual, social, and political needs." They further "called upon totalitarian and oppressive regimes to restore respect for the rights and dignity of the individual and to insure the free and unhindered exercise of these vital rights by all citizens, regardless of racial and ethnic origin, or political or religious espousal." (Quoted in *RES Testimony on Human Rights*, 1983, pp. 36-39.)

Since the turn of the twentieth century, the Orthodox churches of Russia, the Balkans, and Greece have also moved toward a doctrine of separation of church and state. Traditionally, Orthodox churches had taught that civil authorities were God's agents called to govern the "external and temporal affairs" of the church. They thus accepted civil control over many matters of ecclesiastical polity and property. With the rise of an atheistic state in the Soviet Union, a Muslim state in the Balkans, and an increasingly antagonistic state in Greece and Turkey, the church for reason of its own survival has slowly moved in this century to a doctrine of separation of church and state.

The greatest human rights challenge of the Orthodox tradition in the next century will be to help guide the cultural and constitutional reconstruction of post-socialist societies in Eastern Europe and the Commonwealth of Independent States. The fall of the Berlin Wall has brought not only new liberty to these long-closed societies, but it has also brought new license. These societies now face moral degradation, economic dislocation, and human suffering on an unprecedented scale. They face the renewal of ancient animosities among religious and cultural rivals previously kept at bay by a common oppressor. They face a massive influx of foreign missionaries, both religious and economic, offering belief systems and practices that are radically different from those held out by the fallen socialist state and the struggling Orthodox church. A veritable war for souls has thus broken out in the former Soviet bloc—a fight to reclaim the traditional cultural and moral souls of these new societies and a fight to retain adherence and adherents to the ancient Orthodox churches.

The abstract doctrines of modern human rights will have little salience in these societies absent a strong constitution and consistent practice of constitutionalism. Whatever their local forms, these new constitutional developments will profit much from the traditional Orthodox theology of duty-based rights and rights-based social action by the church.

Conclusions

We began our inquiry with the twin legal challenges facing the church in the next century—the challenges that a constrictive state law may pose to the church's ministry, and the challenges that a constructive church ministry may offer to state law. The burgeoning law of human rights provides one effective arena where both these challenges might be effectively met in the next century. A robust rights regime will constrain some of the most intrusive state restrictions on the church. It will contain some of the most fruitful insights and practices that the church has had to offer to the world of law. And, it will sustain some of the most recent expansions of democracy in the new world order.

It must be stressed, however, that a robust regime of human rights and democratic polity will pose its own challenges to the Christian church in the next century. On the one hand, this regime will challenge the *spirit* of the Christian church. Democracy's commitment to religious rights and liberties will open new opportunities to Christianity. Once impervious autocracies will be open to Christian missionaries. Once inaccessible positions of power will be open to Christian influence. As the regime of human rights and democracy expands, it will challenge the Christian church to extend its mission and ministry. On the other hand, this regime's commitment to religious neutrality forces Christianity to fight the "battle of spirits" alone. Historically, state law aided the Christian cause by establishing its doctrines, prescribing its morality, protecting its clergy, subsidizing its proselytes. Human rights and democracy forbid such favoritism. Christianity must stand on its own feet and on an equal footing with all other religions. Its survival and growth must turn on the cogency of its word, not the coercion of the sword, on the faith of its members, not the force of the law. The church is thus challenged to strengthen its sincerity and tenacity.

A regime of human rights and democracy also challenges the *structure* of the Christian church. While the church has preached liberty and equality to the state, it has often perpetuated patriarchy and hierarchy within its own walls. While the church has advocated pluralism and diversity in the public square, it has insisted on orthodoxy and uniformity among its members. The greater the success of the human rights regime, the greater the discordance of such preaching and practice will appear. The same human rights norms that the church has advocated for the state will embolden parishioners to demand greater access to church governance, greater freedom from church discipline, greater latitude in the definition of church doctrine and liturgy. Human rights will challenge the church to restrike its delicate balances between order and liberty, orthodoxy and innovation, dogma and adiaphora.

Christianity, in turn, must challenge the spirit and structure of the regime of human rights and democracy. On the one hand, Christianity must challenge this regime to extend itself. Among current political forms, it holds the most promise for peace, justice, and a better life. It offers the best hope for those who suffer from persecution and penury, discrimination, and deprivation. It affords the greatest freedom to love God, neighbor, and self. Christianity must thus support human rights and democratization in the next century. It must use its collective power and moral suasion to face down autocrats and put down abuse. It must help to break the hardened soils of totalitarianism and sow the seeds of democracy and human rights.

On the other hand, Christianity must challenge the regime of human rights and democracy to reform itself. For all of its virtues, this is far from a perfect political and legal system, far from an earthly form of heavenly government. It is a human creation and inherently flawed. This regime has stored up many idols in its recent life—the proud cults of progress and freedom, the blind beliefs of materialism and technologism, the desperate faiths of agnosticism and nihilism. It has done much to encourage a vulgar industrialization that reduces both human beings and natural resources to fungible and expendable economic units. It has done much to impoverish the already poor, to marginalize the already marginal, to exploit the already exploited. Christianity must work to exorcise the idols of democracy and human rights, to continually drive this regime to reform and renew itself.

Human rights and democracy need such opposition to survive. This regime is an inherently relative system of ideas and institutions. It presupposes the existence of a body of beliefs and values that will constantly shape and reshape it, that will constantly challenge it to improve. "Politicians at international forums may reiterate a thousand times that the basis of the new world order must be universal respect for human rights [and democracy]," Czech President Vaclav Havel declared in 1994 after receiving the Liberty Medal in Philadelphia.

"[B]ut it will mean nothing as long as this imperative does not derive from the respect of the miracle of being, the miracle of the universe, the miracle of nature, the miracle of our own existence. Only someone who submits in the authority of the universal order and of creation, who values the right to be a part of it, and a participant in it, can genuinely value himself and his neighbors, and thus honor their rights as well." (Quoted in *Buffalo News*, July 10, 1994, p. A8.)

Christianity is by no means the only belief system that can meet this challenge. But with a perfect example in the lordship of Christ, and a long tradition of rights ministry at its disposal, Christianity cannot be silent.

BUSINESS LEADERSHIP AND
MORAL IMAGINATION
IN THE TWENTY-FIRST CENTURY

by

Joanne B. Ciulla

Joanne B. Ciulla

Joanne B. Ciulla holds the Coston Family Chair in Leadership and Ethics at the Jepson School of Leadership Studies, the University of Richmond. She is one of the founding faculty of the Jepson School, which is the first school in the world to offer an undergraduate degree in Leadership Studies.

Professor Ciulla has a B.A. from the University of Maryland, an M.A. from the University of Delaware, and a Ph.D. from Temple University. All of her degrees are in philosophy. From 1984-86, she was the Harvard Postdoctoral Fellow in Business and Ethics at the Harvard Business School. Prior to joining the faculty at Richmond, Professor Ciulla taught at the Wharton School, where she had a joint appointment in the departments of Legal Studies and Management. She designed Wharton's first required ethics course for M.B.A. students. She has also held academic appointments at Oxford University, Boston University Graduate School of Business, and La Salle University.

Professor Ciulla has published widely in the areas of leadership studies, international business ethics, and the philosophy of work. She is currently finishing a book about the meaning of work, called Honest Work. *Professor Ciulla is on the editorial boards of* The Journal of Business Ethics, The Business Ethics Quarterly, *and* Business Ethics: A European Review. *She has lectured all over the world and has designed ethics programs for a number of corporations.*

BUSINESS LEADERSHIP AND MORAL IMAGINATION IN THE TWENTY-FIRST CENTURY

by

Joanne B. Ciulla

It is an honor and a pleasure to be part of the Andrew R. Cecil Lectures on Moral Values in a Free Society. My assignment in this year's series on "Moral Values: The Challenge of the Twenty-First Century" is to talk about moral values in a free society and the challenge for business leaders in the twenty-first century. Since this is a weighty subject, I'd like to qualify my remarks. I'm not a business professor, so don't expect to hear about business trends; I'm not a social scientist, so don't expect a discourse on poverty and pollution; and I'm not a theologian, so don't expect God to back me up.

My perspective on this topic is as a philosopher and educator. I also speak as a consultant who has developed corporate programs on ethics and leadership, primarily in the financial services industry. The focus of my presentation is on the issues that need to be addressed in order to educate the next generation of leaders. I will argue that, in order to meet the tumultuous challenges of the twenty-first

147

century, we are going to have to develop moral imagination in business leaders and leaders in all sectors of society. To explore this issue, we'll look at some of the general moral aspects of leadership itself, and then I'll illustrate some of the moral challenges and opportunities business leaders face in their organizations and in international business.

Philosophers have an annoying predilection for splitting hairs on the meanings of statements. I'd first like to clarify the title of this year's series. I don't think that the greatest problems we face in the twenty-first century concern the moral values themselves, but what they mean and how we apply them to identify and solve increasingly complex problems. People don't debate whether honesty is a moral value in business; they debate about what it means when they are engaged in advertising or sales. The public doesn't disagree about preserving human life; in questions of abortion and euthanasia, they disagree about what life is. Liberal moralists in a free society make the mistake of having moral ideals that are so high that they are impractical. Conservative moralists set their standards too low by insisting that ethics is nothing more than following traditional principles and rules. Like all polarized issues, the answer is both: Morality is both high ideals and traditional moral principles and rules. Moral imagination provides the bridge between the idealism of the liberal and the traditionalism of the conservative. It helps us to adapt and apply traditional moral values to unprecedented situations. For example, the traditional medical principle "Do no harm" took on a slightly new meaning when people had to apply it to cases that involved unplugging respirators.

We describe the business world as fast-paced, competitive, changing, and unpredictable. There is a sense in Western democracies that leaders are weak and the sources of authority and values unclear. The world is plagued with crime, terrorism, and genocide in civil wars that are incomprehensible and have no end in sight. Societies denigrate political leaders and distrust business leaders. On the one hand, people everywhere benefit from the watchful eye of the media when news cameras unmask the atrocities of tyrants and the personal improprieties of leaders. On the other hand, all of the information that the media supplies about people makes heroes and positive role models almost impossible. Few people lead lives so morally perfect that they can stand up to the scrutiny of the press. For example, I was distressed to learn that there is even an unflattering documentary on Mother Teresa. In our country, these constant revelations of moral flaws have gotten so bad that I'm beginning to think that the only people who can be leaders are those who have never engaged in sex, politics, or business. Leadership in the twenty-first century promises to be complex and chaotic because of the interdependencies of nations and economies and diversity of the values of followers both inside and outside of the United States. In a diverse and chaotic world, ethics will have to be at the very heart of leadership.

In ancient Greek, *chaos* meant an empty space or an abyss. If there is an abyss today it's the sense people have of a void in society because there doesn't seem to be a shared set of ethical values. Scientists describe chaos as the dynamic relationships of phenomena. A small change in initial conditions can have a large effect on the outcome. The Butterfly Effect notes how the flapping of a butterfly's wings in the Amazon can affect the weather in New York. For example, consider how the actions of a Mexican guerrilla leader could lower the value of the peso, put the American dollar into a free fall, and make it more expensive for us to buy German and Japanese cars and appliances.

We ordinarily use the word chaos to mean confusion, but as we see from the Butterfly Effect, chaos doesn't mean that events are causally disconnected. The mystery of chaos is that a small change at one point in time in one location can have a large effect later. Even when events are connected in a predictable way, you can get unpredictable results. So, in this chaotic world, what does it take to be an effective leader? One role of leaders is to supply people with things they need. Our society seems to lack order, certainty, and a sense of continuity and control over the future. No leader has control over the external forces of politics, economics, or business, nor is it wise in a chaotic world to run an organization as a monolith. In complex institutions such as government, it is foolish to think that leadership will provide a quick fix because other factors such as institutions shape the problems and policies of the country. If people today want leaders who can control chaos, then they are bound to be disappointed. This is one reason why there is wide dissatisfaction with leaders in every segment of American life. Our disillusionment with leaders is not just a problem with leaders, but a problem with followers. Leaders aren't able to control as much as they used to, which means that followers have to control more. A chaotic world requires a new kind of leader and follower. Yet many people still cling to desire for an all-powerful and wise leader who will show them the way.

Plato's Lesson

The problems of people living and working together are problems that recur at different times and in different forms. We can always learn from history. This isn't the first time leaders have confronted a chaotic world. Plato had a lot to say about leadership. Students of leadership often read Plato's *Republic*. In the *Republic*, leaders are philosopher kings who are wise and benevolent. They rule over a stratified society where everyone has a place based on his or her abilities. While there is much to commend the philosopher king, it is hard to imagine him being very effective. It takes more than knowledge of universal forms to lead. While some scholars attack the *Republic* for being a right-wing fascist state, Plato, in depicting the philosopher king, is like the modern liberal moralist—they both err in setting an unreachable ideal. Nonetheless, Plato later changed his view of leadership.

Plato learned about leadership during three disastrous trips to Sicily. The first time, he was invited by the tyrant Dionysius I. Plato was disgusted by the decadent and luxurious lifestyle of Dionysius' court. He returned to Athens, convinced that existing forms of government were corrupt and unstable. Plato then decided to set up the Academy, where he taught for forty years. It was also at this time that he wrote the *Republic*. In the *Republic*, Plato argued that the perfect state could only come about by rationally exploiting the highest qualities in people. Such a state would be led by a philosopher king. Plato firmly believed that the philosopher king could be developed through education.

About twenty-four years after his first visit, Plato was invited back to Syracuse by Dion, who was Dionysius' brother-in-law. By this time Dionysius I was dead. Dion had read the *Republic* and wanted Plato to test his theory of leadership education on

Dionysius' very promising son Dionysius II. This was an offer that Plato couldn't refuse, although he had serious reservations about accepting it. Anyway, the trip was a disaster. Plato's friend Dion was exiled because of court intrigues. Plato left Syracuse in a hurry, despite young Dionysius' pleas for him to stay.

Upon returning to Athens, Plato wrote:

". . . the older I grew, the more I realized how difficult it is to manage a city's affairs rightly. For I saw that it was impossible to do anything without friends and loyal followers. . . . The corruption of written laws and our customs was proceeding at such amazing speed that whereas when I noted these changes and saw how unstable everything was, I became in the end quite dizzy." (Epistle VII, 325c-326.)

Plato, too, saw his world as a chaotic place. Nonetheless he was lured back to Syracuse a third time because Dionysius II promised to make amends with Dion and allow him back into the country. Instead, Dionysius sold all of Dion's property and put Plato under house arrest. Needless to say, when Plato got home from that visit he changed his view of leadership. He lost faith in his belief that people could be perfected. Leaders shared the same human weaknesses as their followers.

In the *Republic*, Plato entertained a pastoral image of the leader as a shepherd to his flock. But after his experiences in Sicily he wrote the *Statesman*, in which he points out that a leader is not at all like a shepherd. Shepherds are obviously quite different from their flock, whereas human leaders are not much different from their followers. Furthermore, people are not sheep; some are meek and cooperative and some are very contentious and stubborn. Hence, Plato's revised view is that leaders are really like weavers. Their main task is to weave together into a society different kinds of people, such as the meek and self-controlled and the brave and impetuous.

If we follow the progression of Plato's work on leadership, he goes from a profound belief that it is possible for some people to be wise and benevolent philosopher kings, to a more modest belief that the real challenge of leadership is getting people who sometimes don't like each other, don't like the leader, and don't want to work together, to work towards a common goal. Jim O'Toole says that leadership is more like being a shepherd to a flock of cats than a flock of sheep.

The *Republic* teaches us the importance of justice and the importance of universal notions of the good. Near the end of the *Statesman*, Plato contends that we can't always depend on leaders to be good, and that is why we need the rule of law. Court decisions on moral issues such as desegregation make the law do what we cannot rely on leaders to do. Good laws serve as substitutes for leadership. They help us to survive leaders with poor moral values. I find the proposal for a balanced budget amendment an interesting case in point. By opposing the passage of such an amendment, are some legislators and members of the public saying that they *do* trust current and future elected leaders to balance the budget?

Business Ethics

An interest in the ethics of business has grown partly in response to deregulation, when the loosening of the rule of law imposed new demands on leadership. In 1981 Peter Drucker said that business ethics was a fad. He called it "ethical chic." Business people from abroad regarded the subject as a typically American form of self-righteousness—the United States had kept the world safe for democracy, and now it was on a mission to save it from unscrupulous business practices. Today things are different. In the past ten years there have been business ethics conferences and forums all over the world, from Moscow to Caracas. Questions about the social and ethical responsibilities of business are not just the concern of a few well-meaning individuals, nor are they the pastime of unemployed philosophers or muckraking journalists. If business ethics is a fad, it's one that keeps popping up in times of change, when people need guidance on how to apply traditional rules or morality to the problems of business. Cicero wrote about unscrupulous business practices in 44 B.C.; the medieval church produced long treatises on the morality of business practices like wage labor, usury, and a fair price; and European social thinkers of the seventeenth and eighteenth centuries engaged in lively debate over the relationship between self-interest and the greatest good. Discussions about ethics and business are not limited to the West. In Tokugawa, Japan, for instance, intellectuals at the Kaitokudo Merchant Academy of Osaka pondered the relationship between business, *keisei* (the order of the social world), and *saimin* (the concept of saving the people).

History tells us that business ethics is a subject that comes and goes. In the 1980s the trend towards various kinds of deregulation in the United States and Europe stimulated an intense interest in the ethics of business and its leaders. Many businesses, particularly in the financial services industries, realized that self-regulation of organizations and the industry was the only way to keep themselves free from the law. In this environment, ethics took on a very important role in business leadership. It was no longer good enough for a business leader to be ethical; he or she had to make sure that moral values were inculcated into the organization. It is arrogant to think that all a CEO has to do is simply *be* ethical. The ethical trickle-down effect is not very dependable in large organizations. Business leaders have to develop and communicate organizational policies and programs that ensure ethical behavior throughout the organization.

Leadership Education

In America, people are disappointed by both leadership *and* the law and, like Plato, the reaction of many educators is to try and prepare future leaders to do a better job. Today we are frustrated not only by ineffective leaders but by immoral ones. Disillusionment with leadership has led to the development of leadership programs in high schools, universities, business, and government. The Jepson School of Leadership Studies is the first school of leadership in the country to offer a bachelor's degree in leadership studies. It was started with a $20 million donation by University of Richmond graduate Bob Jepson. I was one of the four faculty members and two deans who designed the Jepson School curriculum. From the beginning, we realized that the charge of our school went beyond management courses. Leadership is more than a set of techniques.

The purpose of the school was "to educate people for and about leadership." Our mission was "to prepare students to take on the moral responsibilities of leadership." We envisioned all leadership, whether in business, government, communities, or social movements, as service to society. None of us saw the school as an exclusive training ground for future presidents and CEOs. We did not think that everyone could be educated to become a great leader. Students take courses in art, history, and physics, but we don't assume they will all be great artists, historians, or physicists, and the same is true of leadership studies. We had a broader vision of the school as a place where we developed citizens and people who would be capable of taking on formal and informal leadership roles in a business, government, or a community group. If leadership in a free society is like herding a flock of cats, then we not only need to educate the leaders, we need to educate the cats.

Our educational goals coincide with the classical definition of the liberal arts. The liberal arts are those arts that teach people how to live in a free society. In order to educate leaders for a chaotic world, we need all of the liberal arts—from history and literature to science and psychology. In a chaotic world, one of the most important abilities of a leader is to correctly understand current conditions, because as chaos scientists tell us, even with causally determinate systems, any small error in sizing up the initial conditions will lead to unexpected results. In this respect, leadership entails mastery of the fine art of sensing the whole or a broad-based understanding of society as a complex system. Over the past few years, business schools such as Wharton and Harvard have redesigned their MBA programs to include a broader perspective on business through the study of leadership and ethics.

Many large corporations in America also have some sort of leadership development program. These used to be management development programs. Only management today requires more than just math skills or the ten easy lessons listed in boxes and bullet points and shown on overheads. If we are working with complex systems in complex organizations, managers need to have a wider understanding of their work in order to be creative and nimble in the way they manage. It may be just as important for managers to read art history as it is for them to read finance. Most of the latest management books in America have the word *leadership* instead of *management* in the title. This trend does not disparage people who hold management positions; it disparages the old industrial stereotype of the manager who does nothing more than make sure that employees get the job done in some prescribed and orderly way. As leadership scholar Warren Bennis tells us, "Managers do things right and leaders do the right thing."

Earlier I said that in times of chaos, people expect leaders to provide some certainty and order to their worlds. In a chaotic environment, a leader doesn't have perfect control. While leaders cannot offer control over the external environment that affects a company or a society, they can fill the need of followers for stability by being trustworthy. Trust allows people to feel that there is order in their relationship with others. It provides a kind of internal order even when there is no external order. This is why there is so much concern over the ethics of leaders in all walks of life. We want to know and trust our leaders, rather than be dazzled by their power.

Chaos, Trust, and Power

Ethics is central to leadership in a chaotic world. Those who doubt the importance of ethics point to highly effective but unethical leaders of the past and argue that ethics didn't seem relevant to their ability to get the job done. That state of affairs no longer exists. Democratic societies consider force an illegitimate source of power and control. In a chaotic world, there are so many related variables that are affected by so many people that it is difficult to force people to act, whether by the stick or by the carrot. Unlike unethical but effective leaders of the past, it is very hard to keep evil ways secret for long in a society that has an active press, efficient communication systems, and sensible regulations. Sophisticated global telecommunications make it hard for repressive regimes to keep a lid on their dirty secrets. In a free society, a strong set of shared ethical values is an inherently powerful motivator that provides the stability that people need to keep adapting to change.

Our high-tech world has gotten more personal. Access to information makes us feel that we know our leaders better, and because we know them better, we are more concerned about their personal ethics. Information is also power, and information technology equalizes the power of leaders and subordinates. In the past, only the leaders of powerful nations held the tools of destruction; today almost anyone or any group can become a terrorist and create fear and anarchy, as is the case with the Unabomber and in the bombings of the government office in Oklahoma City and the World Trade Center in New York. Power is fragmented and good and evil particularized. Individuals have the capability to do more harm and more good than ever before. The modern world may be more impersonal, but we are more dependent than ever on the ethical integrity of total strangers for our safety and physical well-being. In this environment, the ethics of everyone—leaders and followers, employees and employers—are *really* important.

In order to develop the kind of leaders that we need to be effective in a chaotic world, we have to change the way we think of power. Most organizations use power as a reward. If you do a good job, you move up into a position where you have more power over other people and other people have less power over you. Governments and organizations in the United States and other parts of the world have been on a crash diet. They realize that they have to cut costs and learn to do more with fewer people. The flattening of organizations and the removal of layers of middle managers has made it necessary to give more responsibility to people lower down in organizations. This is one reason why business and government organizations run leadership programs. The power distance between leaders and followers is shrinking.

In business, it is very difficult for people in leadership positions to give up power. Leadership in these flattened organizations requires leaders who are accessible and grant autonomy and at the same time demand that subordinates perform well. Some authors argue that women naturally possess the qualities needed for this new kind of leadership. However, as author Judith Lorber points out, the reason why women tend to be better at this kind of leadership is because they are usually in weaker leadership positions and need the help and goodwill of subordinates, without having the power and re-sources to offer them material rewards. Nowadays, leaders at all levels seem to be in this position. Leaders still use the stick on subordinates, but they have fewer carrots to hand out. They also really need the help of others because of the complex chaotic environment in which all organizations operate.

Recent trends of corporate downsizing resulted in lean and very mean organizations. The buzz words in current management books are *commitment* and *empowerment*. It is a real challenge for business leaders to get commitment from people who work in organizations that by their actions and rhetoric let employees know that they cannot be committed to them. Moral concepts like loyalty and commitment are reciprocal—employees are loyal to companies that are loyal to them. There are also problems with promises of empowerment. After removing layers of management, managers empower lower levels of employees. Sometimes empowerment does not mean a more democratic workplace or more freedom for the employee. It means a greater amount of responsibility for their work rather than the power to control their work. American workers are increasingly cynical about the motivational programs of their employers. The work force of the twenty-first century will be very sophisticated. Business leaders will have to spend less time on motivational techniques that make employees *feel* empowered and more time on the social compact that they have with employees. Most Americans leave their constitutional rights in the parking lot when they go to work. They tolerate that trade-off to earn a living. What Americans don't tolerate is duplicity and manipulation. Business leaders have to have the moral courage to be honest with themselves and their workers about the dynamics of power and authority in their organization.

The challenge of business and political leaders is to build goodwill and consensus in uncertain times. These are necessities because of the changing nature of power. The paradox of consensus is that it is an important value in a free society, but consensus does not always yield the best solutions to problems. Sometimes a moral leader has to go against the wishes of his or her constituents in order to do what is right. Yet, because of the current distrust of leaders and respect for democratic values, many leaders become skittish about doing the morally right thing against the will of the majority.

The problem with dispersion of power in a chaotic environment is that it also disperses responsibility. The economy, not the actions of leaders, is responsible for problems in business. In the enthusiasm to "get government off our backs," it is unclear who will be responsible for what in the future. If everybody is responsible, perhaps no one will be responsible. While the interests of business leaders should be the same as the interests of society, we all know that sometimes they aren't. We should not shrink governmental responsibility over business to the point of withering away its protection of the shared values of our nation. Right now we have more confidence in business leaders than we do the government, but these sentiments go in cycles: We de-regulate and re-regulate.

Personal Morality of Leaders

An inherent part of the ethics of leadership is the way in which a person gets power and the kind of power he or she wields. Leaders have to understand the moral hazards of power for themselves and their subordinates. In every election we try to size up the ethics of the candidates. Unfortunately, we also use ethics as a weapon of political assassination. The most common way that we predict if someone will be an ethical leader is by looking at his or her past. This is a very complicated process because we have to first pick out what facts are relevant and then project those behaviors into future behavior. Unfortunately, the press and the public often choose what is most important on the basis of what is most interesting; this is determined by a kind of telepathy between mass media and the public. Sex is more interesting than legislation, even if it isn't always what is most relevant.

The time frame matters when we make judgments on leaders. What we know now about a job or political candidate's past matters because we try to use that information as a predictor of future success as a leader. History loves a winner and reflects the human inclination to forgiveness. Biographer James MacGregor Burns tells us about the successes of Franklin D. Roosevelt, but he also lets us know about some of Roosevelt's dirty tricks. When we weigh the pluses and minuses in our own minds and consider that it is all in the past, we are willing to forgive and forget the bad and remember the good. We now know that Martin Luther King, Jr., and John F. Kennedy were womanizers. It doesn't seem to matter much looking back. But we don't know whether these scandals would have affected their leadership when they were alive.

When we look at historical accounts of leaders, we have to appreciate the fact that the most ethical leaders in history are often the ones with the greatest amount of moral luck. In a chaotic environment, luck is particularly important. According to philosopher Bernard Williams, some luck is extrinsic and some luck is intrinsic. You need both for success. Intrinsic moral luck is related to intentions and estimates about your ability to succeed at some task. Extrinsic moral luck consists of factors that you cannot control. When faced with difficult ethical problems, we are usually faced with uncertainty of outcome. People can have good intentions (know what the right thing is and why they should do it) but also know that things may not turn out all right. Almost all revered military heroes had moral luck. There are only a few who for the right reasons stormed the hill, did no damage to the enemy, and had all of their men slaughtered. People only become martyrs if they have moral luck after the fact, which is of little comfort to them. Think how one event in history could have changed our view of a leader. What would have happened to Jimmy Carter if the mission to rescue the hostages in Iran had been successful? Carter had, along with other leadership problems, rotten moral luck.

Philosophers have long debated how you judge the morality of people. John Stuart Mill once said that the end of a person's act tells you about the morality of the act. The intentions and the means of doing the act tell you about the morality of the person. This sensible view of morality is very problematic when it comes to leadership. Public discussion concerning the ethics of leaders is sometimes unable to sort the morality of the means and ends of the leader's actions. We tend to over-emphasize leaders as role models, which means that we often demand perfection and are disappointed when we don't get it. We have a strong need for moral leaders whom we can trust, and we want leaders with a track record of doing good things. It is difficult to sort out who is morally good but unlucky, and who is morally shaky but lucky. It all depends on who gets caught and who doesn't. The press recognized this problem when they labeled Reagan the "Teflon President."

The moral foible that the public fears most in a leader is personal immorality accompanied by an abuse of power. Dean Ludwig and Clinton Longenecker call this abuse the Bathsheba Syndrome. In the story of David and Bathsheba we learn how David comes home from the front and, while walking around his palace, happens to see Bathsheba bathing. He seduces Bathsheba and she gets pregnant. King David tries to cover it up by calling her husband home from the front and getting him drunk so that he will sleep with Bathsheba. Her husband won't cooperate because he feels it would be unfair to enjoy himself while his men are still in danger.

The Bathsheba story demonstrates our worst fears about the private morality of leaders. First, we fear that successful leaders will lose strategic focus—David should have been thinking about the war, not watching Bathsheba bathe. This is why we worry about womanizers getting distracted from their jobs. Second, power leads to privileged access. Leaders have more opportunities to indulge themselves. David can have Bathsheba brought to him by his servants—no questions asked. And third, powerful leaders have control over resources, which sometimes gives them an inflated belief in their ability to control outcomes. David gets involved in escalating cover-ups. In the end, he pays dearly for his actions.

The interesting thing about the Bathsheba Syndrome is that it is hard to predict, because people get it *after* they have become successful. It is a reaction to the temptations of power. Someone may have been perfectly ethical in his or her past professional life and then change. Leaders of respected organizations like the United Way and the NAACP were committed activists for their causes but lost their focus and misused their organizations' money and resources once they obtained leadership positions. Similarly, President Richard M. Nixon misused the power of his office to cover up the Watergate break-in. In business there is no greater example of the Bathsheba Syndrome than the outrageous levels of executive compensation. Power is one of the most ethically and emotionally complex parts of leadership and life in general. Leaders have always abused power, but that fact shouldn't stop us from trying to prevent its abuse. Telling these stories to future leaders is one form of moral education because it helps them develop understanding and imagination. That's probably what the writers of the Bible had in mind.

Moral Imagination

Ethical decision making encompasses prescriptive and creative functions. The prescriptive side contains important values, principles, and ideals, such as respect for human life. These principles are explicit and they set certain limits on behavior. The creative part involves the ability to see ethical problems and invent ways to live up to moral prescriptions, given our understanding of a culture and the practical constraints of a situation, such as time and money. Moral imagination also encompasses both the prescriptive and creative elements of morality. I divide moral imagination into *imagining that* and *imagining how*. The prescriptive part of moral imagination includes the ability to imagine *that* a particular situation involves an ethical problem. The concept of *imagining that* is the same as the concept of *seeing as* or *seeing that* or seeing an aspect of something. So one element of moral imagination is the ability to see the ethical aspect of a situation. Seeing and imagining are subject to our will and they require knowledge and memory. I believe that there are some people who lack the capacity to imagine or see the ethical aspects of a situation or problem. I think that this is akin to tone deafness or color blindness. Yet I also think that the ability to see a moral problem is like the ability to see a duck or a rabbit in one of those pictures in which the identity of an object depends on how you look at it and can switch back and forth. We cultivate this ability to see moral problems in the same way that we cultivate a person's ability to appreciate art or music, by showing them how to see and hear.

As with art and music, some people are naturals when it comes to seeing and hearing ethical problems, while others have to learn how to see and listen. In university and management seminars there is always someone who will raise his or her hand and say, with a sigh of relief and satisfaction, that the case doesn't have any ethical problems; there are only management problems. These folks either can't see the ethical problem, don't want to see it, or see the problem but don't want to call it an ethical problem. Experience also tells me that there are people who are just rotten to the core and/or have serious psychological problems. For the ethically blind or ethically tone deaf, we need laws and organizational systems of control.

Imagine That

Additionally, there are two ways that we imagine *that* something is the case. The first involves empathy and seeing what another person and/or culture thinks is ethical and unethical. The second is seeing ethical problems in a particular situation. The increasingly international nature of business requires business leaders to use their imaginations to go beyond the information given to them. Empathy is central to moral imagination. It is more than the ability to put ourselves in another person's shoes. We can do that and imagine how we would feel, but in another culture we have to put ourselves in another person's place and imagine how that person feels, given an entirely different set of values and emotional responses. Empathy requires us to have a strong sense of who we are and what we stand for. Having empathy for someone does not mean that you buy into their value system. You should be able to empathize with Hannibal the Cannibal but still decline his dinner invitation. We also have to beware of falling for the idea that, just because everyone in an industry, organization, or culture appears to engage in a certain practice, that everyone thinks it is ethical.

Of all the places that I have taught seminars on business leadership and ethics, Latin America poses the greatest challenge to my moral imagination. One senses that the line between reality and illusion is very thin at all levels of life. The problem with doing business in Latin America is not conflicting ethical values but a confusing relationship between local values and practices. For example, activities that an American would find unethical, such as bribery, are usually considered unethical by Argentines; the difference is that in Argentina bribery takes place with relative impunity. Nonetheless, when the press reports cases of corruption in Argentina, the public is just as appalled as it is in our country. In some countries bribery is like sex; people know it's done in private, but if you do it in public, you face moral condemnation. *The Economist* reported that a byproduct of corruption in Argentina is an anti-corruption industry. Books about bribery make the best seller list, and schools sponsor competitions for students to devise ways to stop students from cheating.

A similar situation exists in Venezuela. Ruth Capriles, an academic, publisher, and activist, began chronicling corruption scandals in her *Dictionary of Corruption in Venezuela*. Her intention was to make Venezuelans aware of the corruption in business and government in the hopes of creating public pressure for governmental reform. She wanted people to start imagining how these scandals affected them. The dictionary, which is now in its second volume, became a best seller, but Capriles was disappointed with the reaction to her book. Instead of raising consciousness and getting people to rethink their government, the scandals were used as political strategies. Many believe that the dictionary was responsible for the indictment of former president Carlos Andrés Pérez. Capriles recently told me that she thought the problem with Venezuelans was that they had too much imagination, and they preferred to dream dreams that did not take into account the practical considerations. What makes moral imagination different from fantasy or wishful thinking is that it contains truth. Part of truth comes from memory. People, organizations, or countries who do not remember the past suffer from moral amnesia. Part of moral learning comes from our mistakes. Leadership in the brave new world of the twenty-first century had better not forget the tired old world of the twentieth century.

One moral challenge for business leaders is to help other businesses and other cultures imagine morally better ways of doing business. The old injunction, "When in Rome, do as the Romans do," no longer applies. The difference between a Chilean business person and an American one is the Chilean, because he or she is Chilean, cannot fight large-scale corruption on a day-to-day basis. When foreign businesses set up shop in another country, it is very important that they go into the country with a clear sense of identity and organizational values. Ironically, in Latin America any company that could get around paying bribes or facilitating payments would probably be held in higher esteem by the business community than a foreign company that took the easy route and followed local custom. For example, a Chilean colleague told me that when IBM set up shop in Santiago, rather than pay facilitating payments to get all of the necessary permits to set up operations, they made a conspicuous show of standing in lines and going though all of the red tape themselves. This took about ten times as long as it would have taken if they had paid someone to take a shortcut through the system. He said that at first some business people thought IBM's managers were stupid and naive, but after a while, they looked at them in awe. IBM had done something that the others knew was right but could not imagine themselves doing. Hence another moral challenge of business leaders is to make the world the kind of place in which they would want to do business and to help people imagine ways of doing business that are better for business and society. A business leader's moral responsibility is to raise the standard of doing business, rather than stooping to lower standards under the guise of competitive pressure. In this respect, all business leaders can play a transformational role. Yet this does not mean that Americans have nothing to learn from other cultures.

Martin J. Gannon and his associates offer managers another way to understand the values of a culture. In their book *Understanding Global Cultures*, they look at seventeen countries through a culturally representative metaphor. For example, they use the metaphor of the Italian opera to describe Italy. Their discussion is broken into sections on pageantry and spectacle, voice, exteriority (the need to express feelings to others), chorus and soloists, and the family meal. While these are just cultural snapshots, they give a sense of what is generally important to people in a culture, and they form a backdrop of possibilities for creative problem solving.

While it is obvious that learning about history and culture is desirable for business leaders, familiarity with literature is also particularly helpful in developing the capacity for solving ethical problems in morally imaginative ways. Like Gannon's metaphors, literature is able to capture the ambiguities of values of a culture in a way that social scientific studies do not. The reason for this is that a metaphor, analogy, or piece of literature or art helps us understand the ways in which people adapt to these ambiguities because it helps us understand the sentiments behind them. For example, if you want to understand adaptation in Venezuela read the novel *Doña Barbara* by Rómulo Gallegos, García

Marquez's *Autumn of the Patriarch* and *The General in His Labyrinth*, and Isabel Allende's *Eva Luna*. All of these books are about power, inequities, values, and survival against a backdrop of magic and surrealism.

Imagine How

Americans also adapt and repress adverse things in their environment, such as inequality and violence. We sometimes use adaptive behavior to shape the way that we present moral arguments about important issues. People's ethical judgments come from their body, head, and/or heart. They are behaviorally determined (by rewards and punishments), rationally determined, and emotionally determined. This became particularly clear to me when I gave seminars in Europe, Asia, and North America for the top 200 managers of a large Wall Street firm. These seminars consisted of cases that would stimulate discussion of issues facing future leadership of the firm and the industry. The first thing that I noticed was that the company had such a strong organizational culture that, in many of the case discussions, the organization's values and not the local cultural values determined how employees felt about a particular case. This leads one to wonder about the emergence of an international business culture and the moral impact of the values of a multinational business and their impact on a culture's local values.

From the seminars in New York and in other parts of the world, including Japan, I got the most intense discussions about the following case. Your best salesperson has left the company and you have to assign his account, which is the largest account in the office, to someone else. The other top salesperson is a woman. Normally you would simply give the job to her; however, this client has explicitly let it be known that he does not like to work with women. What do you do? The response was interesting when you consider the appearance and reality of the ethical norms of people working in foreign countries. In New York this case caused quite a controversy, especially when women were in the room. If there weren't women in the room, which was most of the time, American men often said, "This isn't an ethical problem; give the account to someone else." If I changed the character to an African American male, the same group was more hesitant in their answers. In the European discussion, someone in the group said that he had faced that question before when dealing with Arabs who didn't want to work with Jews. Then another participant pointed out that Dutch clients didn't like to do business with the Brussels office because they don't like working with the Walloons. What was happening in this discussion was that people began using their imaginations to expand their understanding of what was at stake

in this case. They started to see the slippery slope
of the arguments for not giving the person the job.
All of a sudden the view that "the customer is always right" and the meaning of customer service
took on different lights. Those who started out the
discussion thinking that this was not an ethical
problem began to see that it committed them to
positions that they would not want to hold when it
came to other like problems. We learn about ethics
through experience and analogy of experiences.
Moral learning is a lifelong experience, not something you master as a five-year-old.

In Japan, the discussion took a curious twist.
There were Americans, Europeans, and Japanese in
the room. The Americans were pretty firm about not
giving the account to the woman. However, the
Japanese argued that you had to give the account to
the woman if she was the best person you had.
Democratic concepts such as rights or desert never
entered into their discussion. They simply argued
that the reason why you had to send the woman was
to give the client the best quality service; anything
less would make your business look bad. By the
time I brought the case to Japan, I had already
discussed it with 180 senior managers, and no one
had ever made this particular argument. It too was
a moral argument, based on obligation to the client
and the integrity of the firm. By casting it in a
different set of principles, it defused the difficulty
that American men were having over the emotional-

ly volatile issues of equal rights and opportunities in the workplace. A dialogue like this one drives home an unseen benefit of business in a global economy—the opportunity to gain perspective on our own values and learn new ways to think about ethical problems in business. The strength and weakness of values in a free society come from dialogue and openness to revise the way we understand and use them.

The most difficult problem that business people face everywhere is how to do the right thing without losing a business deal, a client, or money. Imagining *that* focuses on the ability of people to see moral problems. Imagining *how* focuses on creative problem solving. Almost all moral decisions involve risk because we are unable to know for certain how things will turn out. Business leaders have to support moral risk taking and be forgiving of those who make honest mistakes. Earlier, I defined this element of ethics as moral luck. In a perfect world, actions done with good intentions or solid justifications will turn out right, but as we all know, this is not always the case.

Consider the following story told to my class by a student and former businessman who worked for a steel company in India. His company bid on and won the contract for a $20 million project in Venezuela. However, the transaction could not proceed until the Indian government approved the deal. When the Indian government official met with the student, he indicated that all would go well if a $2000 bribe were paid to him. After hearing this part of the story, the class discussed what they would have done in this predicament. Most students felt the bribe request posed an insurmountable barrier to closing the deal. They saw only two incompatible possibilities—either you paid the bribe and got the contract, or you didn't pay the bribe and lost the contract. Arguments for paying the bribe rested on the commonplaceness of bribes in various parts of the world, the size of the transaction, its benefits to India, and the relatively small size of the agent's request.

The first problem with the students' response is that they set up the problem with only two solutions—bribe and make the deal or don't bribe, lose the deal. They could not imagine any other solution. Second, they lacked the confidence and courage to risk losing the deal by not paying the bribe or doing something to avoid paying it. Third, because they had inadequate information about the nature of bribery and Indian culture, they were blocked from a more creative way of presenting the problem.

After a long and heated discussion, the student told the class that he closed the deal. The class, half of which consisted of foreign students, assumed that the bribe was paid. However, the Indian student then said, "Now, let me tell you what I did. That day, I just happened to have my Walkman in my pocket (this was when Walkmen were new). I switched it on and put it on the table. Then I said to the government official, 'I'm sorry, but I forgot to tell you that we tape all of our official conversations with government officials and send them to the appropriate supervisor.'"

The Indian set up the problem in a different way. Because he understood the subtlety of his own culture, he knew that while there was bribery, it was not something you wanted your supervisor to know about. His problem was not whether to bribe or not to bribe, but how to get the official off his back in a way that would save face for everyone involved. His decision was based on cultural understanding, imagination, and the courage to take a risk. But most importantly, the Indian's ingenuity came from a commitment to do the right thing. This particular decision included both adherence and flexibility on moral rules against bribery and lying. Perhaps the most sophisticated level of moral development is being able to identify when it is moral to violate a moral principle.

Some people would seriously object to the Indian's solution. After all, he tricked the government official and he lied. We certainly don't want people to use unethical means to obtain ethical ends. From this perspective, the student did not provide the optimal solution to the problem. But then again, the situation raises a more subtle set of ethical questions about the nature of ethical obligations we have to tell the truth to bribers, terrorists, etc. Some of the most difficult ethical problems we face are those in which there is a conflict of duties and, despite our best efforts, we are unable to do both duties. The student has an ethical obligation to tell the truth and not pay bribes. His solution to the problem requires him to choose between the two, and his choice depends on which duty is more serious in this situation. By using his imagination, the student was able to call the official's bluff, verifying his belief *that* the official's request was not legitimate.

Organizations exercise moral imagination when they turn existing logic upside down and imagine how to create business opportunities that are morally good and make money. One such organization is the South Shore Bank in Chicago. For many years it served a middle class community, but the area turned into a ghetto filled with drugs, gangs, and violence. In 1973 a morally imaginative entrepreneur named Ronald Grzywinski bought the bank for under $4 million. Instead of lending to rich people, he decided that the bank would lend money to the poor and help people rehabilitate their homes and businesses. The bank soon discovered that the poor people in the area were actually much better at paying off loans than some of the rich. Through the South Shore Bank, the neighborhood radically improved. Now it is a livable place with safe streets and a mixed population of whites and blacks. The South Shore Bank is but one example of how morally imaginative leaders can open up a whole new way of thinking for their industry. Not only did it help a community, but it made money. The South Shore Bank's program now serves as a model for banking in neighborhoods and developing countries all over the world. This sort of creativity and moral leadership requires not only imagination but a will and commitment to try to be profitable and make the world better. If business leaders don't try to make the environment that they work in better locally and internationally, it will become more and more difficult for them to do business.

Conclusion

By now you have probably noticed that I haven't said anything shockingly new about the future. This is because when we look at history, we see that the basic moral problems of people living together are not new. Most are just variations on themes, with new actors, props, and stage settings. The props of the twenty-first century are sophisticated information, communication, and transportation systems, and the stage—well, *all* the world *is* the stage. The world has been in a state of chaos before and leaders have abused power in the past. It has also moved forward and backward in terms of moral progress.

American business is more capable of spreading the values of a free society at home and abroad than government. If we are not ethical imperialists, we certainly are cultural imperialists. Business carries the best and worst values of our culture throughout the world in films, TV shows, music, advertisements, and consumer products. It also carries the values of a free society into dialogue with other cultures. We still have a lot to learn from the values and practices of other cultures, just as they have things to learn from us. One way to tell if the values and practices of business are good is if people in other countries find them preferable to their own and more beneficial to their society.

Corrupt leadership probably had more to do with the fall of communism than the attractions of democracy and capitalism. Without communism there are few major critics of the free market. Yet, a quick trip to Moscow will remind you of the wild and seedy side of uncontrolled capitalism. The central moral theme of communism was equitable distribution of goods. Marxist critics are no longer around to remind us that the trickle-down effect is often defective, but we shouldn't forget this criticism. Business leaders will have to keep tinkering with the distribution system because the gap between the rich and poor in America is growing, and some people have too much work while others have too little or none at all. One important moral challenge for business leaders in the twenty-first century is to elevate the standards and playing field of business to the point where there is no industry and no country in the world in which a business-person has to engage in unethical business, labor, or environmental practices in order to be competitive. By improving the ethics of business, we might be able to get the free market system to do what it is supposed to do.

If we continue to shrink the public sector at national, state, and local levels in this country, businesses will have to take up the slack. In the twenty-first century, business will have more social responsibilities than ever before. Companies already find themselves spending millions on remedial education programs and community projects. Leaders of large businesses should include within their strategic focus a variety of variables and responsibilities that go beyond the business itself, but they don't have to. Hence, society will depend on the business community to choose leaders whose moral commitment includes the interests of society.

Our complex world requires leadership at all levels of organizations and society. As I have pointed out, technology, the mass media, and the free market have democratized power by providing people access to information and resources. The measure of good leadership rests on the quality of followers. The quality of followers in a free society is measured by their ability to work together to solve problems; adapt to change; take on leadership roles; assume responsibility for achieving the goals of the group, organization, or community; and demand accountability from the leaders that they choose. Honesty is the only way that leaders will be able to regain the respect 'and goodwill of employees and citizens. It is a key value in a free society, but one that has been undercut by other things such as the desire to be liked (and/or reelected), or the desire to make people feel good, or the desire to make people think they have equal power when they don't. Truth-telling sometimes requires leaders to possess moral courage.

The greatest challenge that business leaders face in the twenty-first century is in their own back yards with their own employees. Today corporate profits are up, executive compensation is up, and working hours per employee are up. At the same time, companies are cutting their payrolls, and workers are watching blue- and white-collar jobs go overseas. Managers offer teamwork and empowerment to their workers and demand loyalty and commitment from them. Meanwhile, employers cut worker's health benefits and freeze salaries. Business leaders have to take an honest look at themselves and assess whether they are being honest with and fair to their employees.

Students of labor history know that unions are famous for rising from the ashes. Union membership moved up 3 percent between 1993 and 1994, reversing a fourteen-year decline. If the new AFL-CIO president, John Sweeney, can remake unions to meet the needs of today's workers, particularly women and workers in the service sector, the twenty-first century could begin with a flurry of organizing activity. Workers are getting fed up with employers who are squeezing them for more work and firing people whenever they get nervous about profits. Employees might be willing to sign on the dotted line if unions offer the right message and use the right approach. Unions and the threat of unions have always forced business leaders to clean up their acts. The morally imaginative business leader will honestly address the issues of justice and fairness before external threats force him or her to do so. Workers in America are unhappy with the arrogance of corporate executives, the losses that they have suffered under the guise of competitiveness, and the unwillingness of business to give them a share in prosperity. There is nothing inherently good about being competitive. What good is a competitive business or economy if it does not improve the lives of employees and citizens? Business leaders have to have the moral imagination to see beyond the numbers in the ledger and make sure that their prosperity is shared by employees and communities. When the stock market booms, the middle class shrinks, and the spiritual and economic poverty of our nation grows, then the values of a free society are in crisis.

We all sense that the pace of change will continue to escalate. The only way that a business will be able to meet competitive challenges in a socially responsible way is to be in a constant state of learning and creating. We need to develop business leaders who are lifelong learners and teachers, able to facilitate learning and imagination in their organizations. From the perspective of moral values in a free society, ethics lies at the heart of leadership. All leaders need to be just and forthright. In a chaotic world, trust in our leaders and confidence in our citizens provides us with a small and fragile island of security, order, and hope. Right now as employees and citizens we stand on shaky ground, and we need to weave ourselves together and work *with* and *on* our leaders to shore up the foundation. As Zen philosopher Fushan Yuan reminds us:

> "Nothing is more essential to leadership and teachership than carefully discerning what to take and what to leave aside. The consummation of taking or leaving is determined within; the beginnings of safety and danger are determined without." (Letter to Master Jingyin Tai.)

And finally, another Zen philosopher, Wuzu, reminds us of the transforming power of moral leadership:

> "As a leader it is essential to be generous with the community while being frugal with oneself. . . . When the community is impressed, things get done even when no orders are given. The wise and the stupid each naturally convey their minds, small and great each exert their effort.

This is more than ten thousand times better than those who cannot help following them, oppressed by compulsion." (Letter to Fojian.)

BEYOND THE HARM PRINCIPLE:
FROM AUTONOMY TO
CIVIC RESPONSIBILITY

by

Bruce Jennings

Bruce Jennings

Bruce Jennings is Executive Director of The Hastings Center, a research and educational institute that studies ethical and social issues in medicine, the life sciences, and the professions. A political scientist by training, Mr. Jennings is a graduate of Yale University (B.A. 1971) and Princeton University (M.A. 1973). He has taught at several colleges and universities and has lectured widely on social, educational, and public policy issues.

At The Hastings Center Mr. Jennings has directed several research projects on professional ethics, health policy, chronic illness, long-term care, and the care of the terminally ill. He served as Associate Director of a project that produced the widely cited and influential Guidelines on the Termination of Life-Sustaining Treatment and the Care of the Dying *(1987).*

Mr. Jennings has written and edited ten books and has published numerous articles on bioethics and public policy issues. He has been a consultant to several governmental and private organizations, including the American Hospital Association, the W. K. Kellogg Foundation, the Prudential Foundation, and the Alzheimer's Association. He currently serves as a member of the Hospital Ethics Committee at the New York Hospital/Cornell Medical Center in New York City.

BEYOND THE HARM PRINCIPLE: FROM AUTONOMY TO CIVIC RESPONSIBILITY

by

Bruce Jennings

"They [the Framers of the Constitution] conferred, as against the government, the right to be let alone—the most comprehensive of rights and the right most valued by civilized men."

—Louis Brandeis (1928)

Born of the ghastly indifference to human rights and dignity that marked the middle decades of our current century, bioethics in its contemporary revival has been the child of liberalism. It has sought, above all, to protect the individual from the overweening powers of professional paternalism and biomedical technology, reminding society that in matters of medicine and the life sciences technical expertise alone has but a limited capacity to provide guidance on the proper ends and uses of our newfound powers. In reshaping how we live and how we die, biomedicine presents no choices that are value-free and few where many values don't conflict. Opposing a spurious positivism and scientism, clarifying and adjudicating value conflicts and choices, and generally resisting overblown claims by professional elites and technocrats to make such decisions without public debate and accountability—these have been the tasks and the terrain of bioethics during the past twenty-five years.

I want to suggest that there is something profoundly right and valuable about all this and also something that has gone, or is threatening to go, terribly awry. In thinking about the problems and fundamental issues to be encountered by bioethics in the twenty-first century and about the role of bioethics in the moral discourse of a free society, one is tempted to adumbrate the agenda of bioethics in reference to the foreseeable technological breakthroughs in the life sciences, principally genetics and molecular biology. With equal cogency, one might point to the widening gap between North and South, the developed and the non-developed worlds, and the health consequences of our global failure to address resource distribution, population control, biodiversity conservation, public health, and sustainable economic growth issues. Then, of course, there are the demographic statistics, which tell us that Western societies and health care systems are going to be preoccupied, at least through the first half of the next century, with the problems of an aging population, an increasing prevalence of chronic illness and disability, and intergenerational conflict over the burden of long-term care.

Is biotechnology a Promethean triumph or a Faustian seduction? How wide is the human moral community and how should sharing take place at its table? And what is the meaning of old age and what is its due? These, I would hazard to guess, will be three prominent topics on the future agenda of bioethics. Yet behind each of them lies a more fundamental question. It, and not specific matters of bioethics and biomedicine *per se*, will be the focus of my reflections here. One way to put the more fundamental question is: How well will liberalism—as a moral framework and a political tradition—cope with these kinds of questions? Another way to put it is: How should freedom be understood and what is its place in the broader human good?

Health, medicine, and the life sciences offer a field of inquiry that is not the only realm in which the philosophical and moral viability of liberalism will be challenged, to be sure, but it is a particularly telling and fecund area for thinking through that challenge. Topics such as biotechnology, global health and ecology, and chronic illness in an aging society are paradigm cases of the clash between freedom and other values because they involve the limitation of pursuits that may bring great power and profit, the redistribution of resources and a declining material standard of living (for those in the North), and a recognition that the need of others may impose a stronger moral claim upon our lives than the inclination of our own desires and interests.

Liberalism, historically, has been inept at handling moral questions such as these. It has been much better at dodging or neutralizing them behind the promises of economic growth and scientific progress. It says: Redistribution is not necessary under conditions of growth because a rising tide lifts all boats. There is no disease without a discoverable cure; even the process of senescence may itself be understood sufficiently that it can be manipulated and bent to our will. We can square the curve of morbidity; we can all live and die like Oliver Wendell Holmes's One-Hoss Shay—we can function perfectly for 100 years and then suddenly disintegrate in an instant.

But these dodges will no longer do. The world's billions will never enjoy the material standard of living of today's average American or German or Japanese. And increasing power to manipulate the body natural no longer impresses itself on our culture as morally praiseworthy "progress." Such advances increasingly will generate social, moral, and spiritual conflicts—not defuse them.

To ask whether bioethics can respond to the challenge of these twenty-first century issues is to ask whether liberalism itself can adapt and respond, for, to repeat what I said earlier, bioethics is a child of liberalism. Bioethics, like liberalism, is largely a discourse about freedom and responsibility, individual self-determination and cultural limits, personal autonomy and social control. Considering the entire history of the liberal tradition from the seventeenth century on, one should say that liberalism has been a reasonably balanced discourse on these subjects. It has, in the work of figures such as Locke, Montesquieu, Tocqueville, and even Mill, certainly recognized the importance of values on the opposite side of freedom's ledger—responsibility, limits, order, and control. Indeed, if it has emphasized the importance of freedom, liberalism has done so not because it takes social order to be unimportant or insignificant, but because it takes it to be all too prevalent, powerful, and ubiquitous. In the political imagination of liberalism, order is more prone to smother than to shred, more likely to dominate than to disintegrate. (The fundamental difference between the liberal and the conservative casts of mind lies precisely in this, I believe.) Thus the liberty of the individual must be shored up with legal protection, political power, and moral argument, particularly against the one locus of order that concerned the early modern liberals above all—the state.

Something began to happen to liberalism in the nineteenth century that has vastly expanded and accelerated in the last thirty years. Political liberalism has become social liberalism. The liberal idea of freedom has been given a distinctively libertarian interpretation as the concept of "autonomy." The traditional liberal suspicion about governmental control has been turned into a generalized contemporary suspicion of all forms of social or interpersonal control or restraint blocking the subjective will, the existential "projects," or the "life plans" of the self.

Bioethics has followed—and contributed in no small measure to—this libertarian turn within liberalism and has helped to produce what I shall refer to by way of shorthand as the "culture of autonomy." I believe that bioethics in the next century must retrace its steps and critically reassess this libertarian turn. If the moral and social challenges posed by health, medicine, and biotechnology are to be met, bioethics must recover—and must articulate anew—a conception of freedom that is more civic and communal in orientation than autonomy or a libertarian conception of freedom. Bioethics must not accept the culture of autonomy on its own terms but must confront that culture with an ethical discourse well attuned to the human and moral significance of interdependency, mutuality, and reciprocity. In particular, bioethics must explore the moral justification of state action and social coercion with a broader framework than that offered by autonomy liberalism, which is able to politically motivate and to ethically justify restriction of individual choice only in order to prevent harm to others.

My aim in this lecture is to explore moral terrain beyond the harm principle. To do so, I will take up three topics. First, I will probe the meaning of autonomy and the sources of its appeal. Second, using as an example the controversy over environmental tobacco smoke as a health hazard, I will examine the logic and the limits of the harm principle in bioethics and liberal argument. Finally, I will sketch at least an outline of what an ethic of interdependency and civic responsibility would look like.

The Culture of Autonomy

A misguided assumption stands behind most public policy debate in America. It is that society can and should rely primarily on self-interested incentives and rational moral commitments to achieve cooperation and maintain what jurists call "a system of ordered liberty." From birth control to parking tickets, from waste recycling to cycling with helmets, the American inclination is to prefer persuasion and voluntary compliance. When coercive policies are enacted, they are often not vigorously enforced, or their enforcement slacks off when the momentary crisis or public uproar fades.

Moreover, this point of view tries to eschew internal sources of restraint and coercion as much as it disdains external sources of constraint. Autonomous self-restraint should be enlightened and principled. It should not be based on emotions, prereflective habits, or traditions. In the culture of autonomy, moral progress consists in leaving behind a conscience built on shame, guilt, and pride, for these social emotions belong to the childhood of the race. Ideally, social order should be maintained by self-control based on rational persuasion, deliberation, and reflective commitments to agreed-upon moral principles, rules, and rights. Thomas Hobbes, who had no faith whatsoever in the possibility of building social order on the basis of reason alone, rejected the social emotions because he thought they were too weak, and turned instead to the primitive emotions, saying with his usual terseness, "The passion to be reckoned on is fear." Standing Hobbes completely on his head, modern-day proponents of autonomy urge society to "transcend" norms based on the psychology of the ego, and to do "without guilt and justice." In short, the culture of autonomy assumes that social order can be maintained principally on the basis of rationally persuasive appeals to self-interest and to consciously chosen moral values. And it assumes that living a life that is freely chosen and autonomous in this sense epitomizes the good life for the individual, while a society composed of lives lived freely is the good society.

This is a vain illusion, and not even a very attractive one if it is examined closely. I, for one, am grateful for moral behavior based on sentiment and don't think it any the worse for that. The autonomy position seems to me to be as mistaken and one-sided as the view propounded by deterministic behaviorists, who insist that autonomy-inspired con-

ceptions of individual freedom and dignity are obso-
lete.

Two main objections can be raised against autonomy liberalism. One is a prudential or political
argument. It is that the culture of autonomy does
not provide us with adequate means of justifying
social control and coercion when they are needed.
Although autonomy liberalism does offer a way
ethically to justify coercion and social control, it is
too limited in the range of moral reasons it offers
and too restrictive in the modes of social control it
will permit. We must go beyond the discourse of
autonomy in order to justify social control in a way
that better meets our social needs. And we must
find the necessary concepts and arguments—an
alternative vocabulary of relationship, responsibility, duty, and the common good—to do so.

The second objection is a moral and philosophical one. It is that autonomy does not provide an
acceptable moral understanding of the human good
or of the fabric of our lives as moral beings. The
aspiration for mankind to outgrow the need for
feelings of shame, guilt, and pride is both biologi-
cally and psychologically unrealistic, since these
psychological capacities are the product of human
evolution and the byproducts of the fact that our
behavior is relatively unshaped by instinct and
largely shaped by social and cultural processes of
identity formation. But the important point here is

not so much that autonomy's dream is psychologically unrealistic. Equally important is the fact that
it is ethically and philosophically inadequate. To
slough off the social emotions in favor of rational
self-interest and commitments voluntarily chosen
would be to exist apart from the web of interdependency and relationships that makes up the warp
and woof of human moral existence.

The social emotions are not symptoms of moral
childishness, they are the signs of moral engage-
ment, embeddedness, and maturity. Persons without
shame, guilt, pride, and conscience are not to that
extent admirable, they are morally malformed. That
is nothing to celebrate. And in a culture and social
order that deliberately and systematically tries to
produce such people, there is little to praise.

Autonomy comes from the Greek *autos* (meaning
self) and *nomos* (meaning rule, governance, or
law). Literally, therefore, autonomy means the state
of being self-governed or self-sovereign; living
autonomously means living by a law that you impose on yourself. In other words, autonomy is the
right to live your own life in your own way. The
original usage of the term was political and referred
to the self-governing ancient Greek city-state.
Cities had *autonomia* when they made their own
laws and controlled their own affairs, as opposed to
being controlled by some other city or empire. Over
time, particularly in the writings of the eighteenth-

century German philosopher Immanuel Kant, the term has also been applied to ethics and to the individual person. Kant talked mainly about autonomy of the will or intention, while a generation later the English philosopher, John Stuart Mill, talked mainly about autonomous action and choice. Both Kant and Mill have had a tremendous influence on contemporary liberalism.

These old ideas are still current. One widely used college ethics textbook teaches students that autonomy is the "personal rule of the self that is free from both controlling interferences by others and from personal limitations that prevent meaningful choice. . . . The autonomous individual freely acts in accordance with a self-chosen plan . . . ." (Tom Beauchamp and James Childress, *Principles of Biomedical Ethics*, Oxford University Press, 1994, p. 121.)

Other philosophers and psychologists, such as R.S. Peters and Lawrence Kohlberg, say that autonomy requires a deliberate self-consciousness about obedience to rules. They place it at the pinnacle of moral development. Peters stresses rational deliberation about the validity of rules. For his part, Kohlberg also pictures the best moral agent as standing judgmentally above the existing rules, laws, traditions, habits, and norms of his society and choosing with rational detachment which rules to follow and which to disregard.

Lawrence Haworth, author of one of the few
book-length studies of the concept of autonomy,
defines autonomy as having what he calls "critical
competence." "Having critical *competence*," he
writes, "a person is first of all active and in his
activity succeeds in giving effect to his intentions.
Having *critical* competence, the active person is
sensitive to the results of his own deliberation; his
activity is guided by purposes he has thought
through and found reasons of his own for pursuing." (*Autonomy*, Yale University Press, 1986, p.
46.)

Like so many English words that derive from
ancient Greek or Latin, *autonomy* has a stuffy and
legalistic air about it. Philosophers may use it a lot,
but ordinary people don't. It's a word seemingly
more at home in a courtroom or in a congressional
hearing than on a talk radio program, around the
dinner table in the suburbs, or over open lunch
boxes at a construction site. Don't be misled. While
the *word* autonomy is not often used in everyday
conversation, the *idea* it stands for is everywhere.
Americans live, breathe, and dream autonomy. It is
the mark of success in life; it is what we reward
and admire in others and strive for in ourselves.

The autonomy of the individual is America's
greatest moral strength and its most insidious moral
danger. The United States features history's longest
running democratic experiment, now well into its

third century, and our greatest achievement so far has not been peace nor even material prosperity but the unprecedented measure of autonomy we give to individuals in their lives. Autonomy's stock is on the rise with ordinary people, and not just academic intellectuals. It has been boosted (some would say bloated) by the various human and civil rights movements prominent since the 1960s: civil rights for racial minorities, women's rights, abortion rights, gay rights, consumer rights, even patients' rights and the right to die. Paternalism—making someone do what is good for him even if he doesn't want to—is much out of favor; we mistrust paternalistic professionals like doctors and other experts, and at least large majorities of middle-class voters want paternalistic government off our backs. Some children now sue and "divorce" their parents, so it may not be long until even parents won't be able to get away with paternalism.

Autonomy is further reinforced by many powerful movements in the 1990s that are on the right wing of the ideological spectrum—economic conservatives who extol the virtues of free market competition, philosophical libertarians who defend private property rights and resist government taxes, and, most uncompromising of all, militant anarchists (like the numerous citizen militia groups) who pretty much deny any form of governmental or social authority. These latter-day anarchists make liberal defenders of autonomy mighty nervous, it is true, but it is impossible to deny that the value placed on personal autonomy is one powerful motivating factor behind the anti-government mood that is sweeping the country at the grassroots level today. The right-wing militias are simply the most extreme manifestation of that mood.

In a thoughtful article on the ideology and ethos of right-wing militia groups, Denis Johnson relates his own gut-wrenching fascination with the independence and self-reliance these groups symbolize and idolize. Having become acquainted with members of the movement in Alaska, Johnson was invited to spend his honeymoon at a remote site in the Bonanza Hills southwest of Anchorage. The way Johnson describes his experience gives a good feel for the street-level meaning of autonomy:

> "My wife and I honeymooned that month at David's mining operation in the Bonanza Hills. A plane dropped us off . . . [and] Cindy and I lived without any contact with what I had up to then believed to be the world, in a place without human community, authority, or law, seventy miles from the nearest person. . . . [T]hings I'd never thought about became uppermost: matches and tools and, above all, clarity of thought and the ability to improvise. We had to stay focused in our senses, ever mindful of our tasks, because what we'd brought and who we were was all we

had. At last, whatever happened to us could only be *our* fault or bad fortune, and fixing it *our* responsibility. We realized our lives had never before been our own—*our* lives. I had always lived under the protection of what I've since heard called 'The Nanny State': Big Mom, ready to patch me up, bail me out, calm me down, and only a three-digit phone call away.

"Just the same, it's a free country. I'd always taken for granted that the government looked after the basics and left me free to enjoy my liberty. Now I wasn't so sure. This little taste of real autonomy excited in me a craving for it. Maybe I wanted freedom from the government's care and protection. Maybe I wanted freedom from any government at all. I felt grateful for people like David, who'd run away from home and could get along for weeks at a time in a place like the Bonanza Hills." ("The Militia in Me," *Esquire*, July 1995, p. 40.)

To be master of yourself is to belong to yourself. Denis Johnson captures this idea nicely with his use of the possessive pronoun to express the exhilaration he felt when it dawned on him and his wife alone in the wilderness that "who we were was all we had. . . . We realized our lives had never before been our own—*our* lives."

This self-mastery carries with it a tremendous sense of capability, and a surge of responsibility.

But the responsibility here is an individualistic concept, not a social one. It is responsibility *for* oneself and what one does, not a responsibility *to* others. Social duty, like the rest of society, is absent from the moral world of the Bonanza Hills camp. The responsibility felt there is a lonely one; Denis and Cindy are responsible in the sense that if something goes wrong, they have no one else to blame. It is interesting that in his account Johnson places himself in the company of his wife. He is not alone, but he might as well be. He makes the couple into a single self by essentially engulfing her identity into his own. He uses the first person plural, but it is the first person singular that is heard. There is a vexing thing about autonomy as self-mastery: it's hard to share.

A powerful expression of autonomy as self-mastery is explored in Toni Morrison's stunning novel, *Beloved*. Morrison writes of the experience of freedom first sensed by Baby Suggs, matriarch of the family whose deeply scarred life the novel examines, when her freedom is purchased from a sympathetic master by her slave son, Halle, and she crosses the river from Sweet Home plantation in Kentucky into southern Ohio:

"When Mr. Garner agreed to the arrangements with Halle, and when Halle looked like it meant more to him that she go free than anything in the world, she let herself be taken 'cross the river.

. . . What for? What does a sixty-odd-year-old slavewoman who walks like a three-legged dog need freedom for? And when she stepped foot on free ground she could not believe that Halle knew what she didn't; that Halle, who had never drawn one free breath, knew that there was nothing like it in this world. It scared her. "Something's the matter. What's the matter? What's the matter? she asked herself. She didn't know what she looked like and was not curious. But suddenly she saw her hands and thought with a clarity as simple as it was dazzling, 'These hands belong to me. These *my* hands.' Next she felt a knocking in her chest and discovered something else new: her own heartbeat. Had it been there all along? This pounding thing? She felt like a fool and began to laugh out loud." (Penguin, 1988, p. 141.)

Autonomy as self-mastery has taken up permanent residence in our modern moral imagination. Once you have crossed with Baby Suggs to the north bank of the Ohio, there is no turning back.

And if we can't turn back, we also can't—or shouldn't—understate what the idea of autonomy as self-mastery implies. Many Americans do think of autonomy as choice for its own sake, but as a philosophical understanding of the meaning and value of autonomy, this is not adequate. Self-mastery means

something more than "do your own thing." Halle
and Baby Suggs knew this. Self-mastery is not just
a hollow shell that Baby Suggs could then fill with
her own subjective values, plans, and life-style
choices. As an unblinking observer of being black
in America, Toni Morrison has no time, and less
patience, for such notions. Arriving on the "free"
soil of southern Ohio in the days before the Civil
War, Baby Suggs had no equality and precious little
opportunity and was far too old and tired to be
filling up empty jugs of autonomy with her freely
chosen life plans. The kind of experience Morrison
is talking about when Baby Suggs discovers self-
mastery is not something Baby Suggs has to fill, it
is something that fills her. It transforms and re-
creates her anew, paradoxically by letting her discover a self that was there all along. There, but
obscured and concealed by the weight of slavery,
which is not only a set of laws, practices, and
power relationships, but also a prison house of
images, symbols, defenses, deceptions. Ideas matter. The poet William Blake called ideas such as
slavery "mind-forged manacles." It is a necessary
good for a human being to rise above them so that
you can see yourself plain and be yourself truly.

The culture of autonomy has deep roots and
many branches. It has emerged gradually out of the
underlying forces of individualism, secularization,
materialism, and rationalism that have defined

modernity itself in the West. It has become a guiding principle and an explicit moral ideal in the ideologies of liberalism and capitalism, and it has achieved refined expression in some of the most influential works of moral philosophy, political theory, and literature since the French Revolution. Finally, during the past thirty years or so, the culture of autonomy has truly coalesced into the predominant sensibility and outlook in the United States.

This was not always true in the past, although Americans have always been an unusually individualistic and anti-authoritarian people. But to recognize that it has become true is the most illuminating and suggestive way to make sense of what has happened to culture and politics in the United States in the past three decades. In this plural, cacophonous society, autonomy is the *lingua franca*. At a time when everything is hyphenated, from married names to political loyalties, when all tickets are split, all bets hedged, and all genders ambiguous, autonomy is the one bandwagon everyone can climb aboard. It is the one goal that remains on the list after we have eliminated all the other values and beliefs once thought to be matters of common ground or shared purpose in America, but are no more.

Autonomy has bored deeply into the laws of the land through thirty years of jurisprudence and legislation that has weakened state authority and

strengthened individual rights, privacy, and en-
titlements. Autonomy has penetrated no less deeply
into the everyday lives of people when it becomes
—as it has to a large extent—the moral yardstick
used to evaluate how others treat us and how satisfying and successful our own lives and careers are.
When people feel or experience relationships as
encroachments, disciplined activity as a straight-
jacket confining self-expression, or duties as mill-
stones around their necks, that is the seductive
voice of autonomy whispering in the heart. When
people support public policies and social practices
that maximize personal freedom of choice, no
matter what the moral or financial cost to society
and no matter how self-destructive the behavior in
question, that is the seduction of autonomy as well,
speaking as an ideological dogma in the congregation of libertarianism, left and right. Autonomy is
a very powerful and liberating idea. It is also a
very solitary and negative way to live.

It is important that society not be turned into
Society, with a capital S, and elevated into some
overarching entity that is supposedly superior to,
and is pitted against, the individual as such. There
has been quite enough of that kind of thinking already in the twentieth century. The conditions of
human flourishing cannot be imposed from above,
and they cannot be restored merely through the
reassertion of traditional forms of belief or authority. Those conditions must come from both feeling

and reason, both imagination and intellect. They come from forces that reflect things larger and older than our autonomous egos—drives acquired in human evolution, tradition, the moral law expressed through the forgotten faces and voices of fathers and mothers. And, let us not forget, these conditions of human flourishing rely on the deliberate commitments each individual makes as a moral agent, as a unique, individual self. These conditions cannot be sustained unless we reach for moral ideals beyond autonomy and unless we limit autonomy in the name of these ideals in certain instances. But neither can they be sustained by circumventing autonomy altogether. We must learn to use coercion for the sake of autonomy, and appeal to autonomy to reach for a form of moral life richer than autonomy alone.

I say this in a deliberately paradoxical way. I do so because I believe that the basic moral project facing America today is the paradoxical one of combining seeming opposites. Our human moral condition resembles the Roman god Janus, who had two faces looking in opposite directions. Human beings are Janus-faced creatures by nature, and it is in a Janus-like social and moral world where they are most humanly at home. There have been other societies, past and present, existentially simpler than ours; they gaze at a single horizon. But I do not believe that they were superior. Individual human beings are both independent and dependent or interdependent. They can rise above the givens of their historical time and place via critical intelligence and imagination and yet their thoughts and feelings are socially encumbered and trapped in the prison house of language. The individual's moral identity is now recognized to be made up of rights and negative liberties, and we can't turn back the clock on that even if we wanted to. Yet these freedoms have no meaning apart from the living of a life that is caught up in positive obligations, responsibilities, and relationships.

Conservative critics of autonomy make a mistake when they embrace only forms of social control, authority, and coercion that limit individual choice. Or when they penalize those forms of behavior that violate traditional moral rules and virtues, and leave it at that. What this overlooks is that it is necessary to promote as well as protect the social conditions of human flourishing. The power of social institutions and resources should be used to influence and control behavior, not only in order to deter socially destructive and morally wrong conduct, but also to enable constructive, responsible conduct.

If one is concerned about the destruction of relationships of mutual commitment and responsibility in the family, then one must look to the corrosive, disruptive effects of the market system as well as the perverse incentives built into the welfare state. If one is concerned about the devastating psychological effects on children of inadequate parenting and early childhood stimulation by adult caregivers, then one must promote adequate public funding and regulation for day-care centers and generous corporate parental leave policies, as exist in Scandinavian countries, as well as take vigorous steps to discourage teen pregnancy and to break the vicious cycle of multigenerational AFDC dependency.

If one is concerned about the degradation of our urban environment by homeless men, vagrancy, and aggressive panhandling, then one must look at the utter failure of government to fund adequate community-based treatment facilities for mental illness and halfway houses for drug rehabilitation as well as at the excesses of civil libertarian advocates and the courts in extending the rights of the mentally ill to the point where institutional confinement, even when it is manifestly in the best interest of the patient and society, is virtually impossible. Homelessness as it has plagued our society in the 1980s and 1990s has grown out of an unholy alliance between civil libertarian advocacy for individual autonomy and a brand of fiscal conservatism and anti-government ideology that supported deinstitutionalization because it saved money, but blocked adequate public funding for community-based programs. The result has been a social and a moral catastrophe.

To mention one final example, if one is opposed to the legalization of physician-assisted suicide and euthanasia, then it isn't enough simply to reaffirm and support existing laws against homicide and assisted suicide; it is incumbent upon us to improve the system of hospice care, pain treatment, and palliative care and to eliminate as much as possible the dehumanizing aspects of the way our medical system cares for people at the end of their lives.

The Harm Principle and Negative Liberty

Does autonomy provide a moral basis for its own curtailment? To an extent—and in characteristically individualistic ways. Autonomy does not entail the political philosophy called anarchism, although many strongly libertarian defenders of autonomy, such as Robert Paul Wolff and Robert Nozick, come close to it. Political anarchism is the doctrine that no state or government can be morally justified, and social anarchism goes one step further and holds that no coercive social or cultural pressures should ever be imposed on the individual, either. For anarchists, human beings are naturally free and autonomous; they have natural rights to life, liberty, and property that no social institution or majority can rightfully take away. States and governments have arisen historically to enslave people, and political power has always been imposed.

The concept of autonomy that is most influential in the United States today is an offshoot of liberalism, not anarchism. For liberals, state and social authority can be morally justified, and some means of social control can rightly override the autonomy of the individual under certain limited circumstances. While practically significant, the philosophical difference between liberalism and anarchism is not all that great. It comes down basically to different empirical assumptions about what is historically likely and possible. Anarchists are optimists about human nature. They believe that people can in fact achieve voluntary and spontaneous harmony and cooperation. Crime, poverty, and other sources of conflict arise because of the unnatural and corrupting conditions created by political authority itself and its corresponding social inequality. Hence the conflict that most people think makes the state necessary is actually caused by that very remedy; abolish the state and the need for it will wither away.

Liberals are pessimists on this score. "The latent causes of faction [conflict] are . . . sown in the nature of man," says James Madison in *Federalist No. 10*, expressing a classic liberal position. Left to their own devices, individuals will violate one another's rights, and various political and social controls are necessary to keep interactions within the bounds of justice and to direct human activity

and energy into cooperative and constructive chan-
nels. However, like their anarchist cousins, liberals
want to maximize the sphere of autonomous choice
and to minimize the power of the state. As the
culture of autonomy has developed in recent years,
it has gone beyond the traditional liberal concern
about limiting state interference in the life of the
individual and has extended those limits to include
interference in all the spheres of society, including
civil society and the family. The problem for liberalism, then, has been to find a basis for the moral
justification of political and social control that
adequately sustains social order while at the same
time giving individual freedom of choice, self-
determination, and self-sovereignty—in a word,
autonomy—as much free rein as possible.

The definitive solution to this problem, for traditional liberalism and for the later culture of autonomy, was given by John Stuart Mill in his book *On
Liberty*. "One very simple principle," Mill argued,
is

"... entitled to govern absolutely the dealings
of society with the individual in the way of
compulsion and control, whether the means used
be physical force in the form of legal penalties
or the moral coercion of public opinion. That
principle is that the sole end for which mankind
are warranted, individually or collectively, in

interfering with the liberty of action of any of their number is self-protection. That the only purpose for which power can be rightfully exercised over any member of a civilized community, against his will, is to prevent harm to others. His own good, either physical or moral, is not sufficient warrant. He cannot rightfully be compelled to do or forbear because it will be better for him to do so, because it will make him happier, because, in the opinions of others, to do so would be wise or even right. These are good reasons for remonstrating with him, or reasoning with, or persuading him, or entreating him, but not for compelling him or visiting him with any evil in case he do otherwise. To justify that, the conduct from which it is desired to deter him must be calculated to produce evil to someone else. The only part of the conduct of anyone for which he is amenable to society is that which concerns others. In the part which merely concerns himself, his independence is, of right, absolute. Over himself, over his own body and mind, the individual is sovereign." (*On Liberty*, Bobbs Merrill, 1958, p. 13.)

Constraining the autonomy of the individual is morally justified by the culture of autonomy only when doing so is necessary to protect other individuals from involuntary harm or to protect the negative liberty of other individuals. That, in a nutshell, is the up-to-date version of Mill's answer. This is now commonly referred to as the "harm principle." Preventing harm to others is virtually the only thing that can be used to justify coercive interference to limit the freedom of choice of an autonomous adult.

How does the harm principle work in practice? Everything revolves around how harm is defined, who defines it, and what criteria are used. Sometimes the notion of harm seems to get stretched in order that certain forms of behavior can be curtailed and overriding autonomy can be justified when there is sufficient social or political pressure to do so. In New Jersey, the state Supreme Court recently upheld the so-called Megan Law, which requires public disclosure of the address of previously convicted sex offenders when they are released from prison and move into a community in the state. Here the notion is that the privacy of these individuals should be subordinated in order to protect the community from the harm or the threat of not knowing that a convicted sex offender or child molester is living in their midst. Is this a harm to the community? Perhaps, but if we define harm this broadly, where would disclosure of risk stop?

Another example is provided by a local ordinance in Indianapolis and in the new Canadian constitution, the *Charter of Rights and Freedoms*. These laws ban pornography, not on the traditional grounds that it violates community morality, but on the grounds that pornographic images and speech are harmful and discriminatory *per se* to women. Anti-hate speech codes and rules on many college campuses are based on analogous notions of discrimination and harm. Yet another example is the extraordinary nationwide campaign against smoking in public places, justified by the harm caused by environmental cigarette smoke, to which I will turn in a moment.

Other things that might seem, on the basis of common sense, to be harms, are not so construed by the courts or by defenders of autonomy. One notorious example was the affirmation some years ago of the right of American Nazis to march in Skokie, Illinois—a community in which many Jewish survivors of the Holocaust reside. Its support for autonomy and freedom of expression in that case nearly tore the American Civil Liberties Union apart. How grave does offense have to be before it becomes harm? Pictures of exposed genitalia in Indianapolis are grave enough, but swastikas and brown shirts in Skokie aren't, apparently.

Consider another, quite different, example. Members of the religious community called Jehovah's Witnesses are forbidden by their faith from receiving blood transfusions and are often willing to die rather than do so. In recent years, the courts have affirmed the right of adult Witnesses to refuse lifesaving transfusions. The only limitation placed on this autonomy is the welfare of minor children. If the person refusing treatment is a single parent and there is no one else to care for the children, then perhaps a court might order treatment. This rarely happens. The Witnesses are a close-knit community, and someone is always found to take in the child. The effect of a parent's (easily preventable) death on a young child is not considered a "harm." Call it what you will—a tragedy, a wound, a trauma, a loss too deep for words—it is not a harm powerful enough to trump autonomy (in this case, freedom of religion) in our moral universe today.

Similarly, some would argue that the harm principle should be invoked to limit the autonomy of pregnant women due to concerns about the health or well-being of the unborn fetus. But when the question has been raised, the courts have rather consistently come down on the side of women's autonomy rather than protection of the fetus. Even so, a moral sensibility in which responsibility supersedes autonomy remains a strong undercurrent in this highly charged area. Informal pressures abound and various attempts to influence pregnant women's behavior continue to be made, in spite of their questionable legal status. Signs in public taverns warn pregnant women not to drink, and there have been instances where waiters or bartenders have refused to serve them. Social pressures and adverse reactions, even from strangers, are beginning to mount on pregnant women who smoke. Medical coercion and even legal sanctions were used as part of the drug counseling policy in the prenatal clinic at the Medical University of South Carolina. Fearing lawsuits and avowing a concern for the unborn, some corporations have tried to adopt policies that exclude women factory workers who could not prove that they were infertile from certain high paying jobs because they could be exposed to chemicals that would not harm their own health but would harm their fetus. These policies, like the one at MUSC, have been overturned by the courts.

There is much irony and bitter social controversy when the harm principle is invoked against the autonomy and free choice of a pregnant (or even fertile) woman on behalf of her unborn child. For one thing, the harm principle has an impact only on those women who choose not to exercise their autonomous legal right to terminate their pregnancy. Much, if not all, of the abortion debate since the *Roe v. Wade* decision of 1972 has taken place within the intellectual framework of liberal autonomy and the harm principle. Basically, the effect of *Roe* was to hold that until the point of fetal viability the harm principle does not apply because the pre-viable fetus is not a person whom the Constitution (or our public morality) must protect from harm. Opponents of legal abortion who do believe that the fetus is a "person"—or at any rate, a human being, a member of the human moral community and deserving of protection—can use the harm principle to override the autonomy of a woman in straightforward liberal fashion. Anti-abortion advocates sometimes do use this liberal terminology, although, of course, other religious and moral ideas, not all of which are compatible with liberalism, undergird their arguments as well.

Still, the liberal framework of autonomy and the harm principle does give both pro-choice and pro-life sides of the abortion debate a common reference point, and they come to opposite conclusions within the same logic of ideas because they disagree on the status of the being (the fetus) on whose behalf the harm principle limiting autonomy is to be invoked. It is telling that rarely, if ever, in this debate has the harm principle been invoked on behalf of someone besides the fetus. We rarely talk about fathers here since, in the individualistic moral universe of autonomy, relationships (even if they exist) morally don't matter. And we rarely talk about what effect the practice of abortion (or the practice of banning abortions and coercing women) has on the character and texture of our lives together in a moral community. Contexts of cultural meaning and social relationship are venues in which we form intentions, shape identities, and exercise moral agency. But they are not morally significant things or objects of value in the culture of autonomy. They fall within its moral blind spot.

Mill's "simple principle" should make the use of coercion and social control in a liberal society an intellectually neat and tidy affair. It is anything but. The harm principle ought to give us a bright line to know when individual autonomy can be overridden. The line is not really so bright, however, because people don't always know harm when they see it, or else they see it too readily when it is not reasonably there. The culture of autonomy forces civic discourse and ethical argument about social control into the narrow confines of two questions. First, what is harm? How narrowly or how broadly, and how objectively or subjectively, should harm be defined? Second, when is harm really harmful? That is, should the state override autonomy only to protect people from harm (or risk of harm) that is involuntary, or should it also protect people from harm to which they voluntarily expose themselves?

The definition of harm is a crucial question and a thorny problem for public policy. Define harm too expansively and autonomy shrinks. How serious does harm have to be? Is it only serious physical harm or injury, or does psychological damage, pain, and suffering count as well? What is the gradation between harm, offense, annoyance, and inconvenience? Where should we draw the line? Over time the culture of autonomy has tried to resolve these quandaries by interpreting "harm" in terms of negative liberty and negative rights. Harms are those things that encroach on my private space, those things that I don't invite in. I am not harmed by things that other people omit to do, I am harmed by what they commit—what they do directly to me. Protecting me from harm, therefore, means protecting me from outside interference, from unwanted or uninvited contact, from those who would place barriers in my path. These are the "freedom froms" of autonomy as negative liberty. To argue first that social control can be morally justified only in order to protect individuals from harm, and then to define harm as the violation of negative liberty, is to deploy the resources of social control predominantly in order to keep people apart. Privacy trumps commitment, connection, and relationship. But should it? Why must society's power always be used to build walls and never to tear them down?

Interpreting harm as a violation of negative liberty also leads to a subjective definition of harm so that, in effect, the notion of a voluntary harm is a contradiction in terms. For the most part, the harm principle has been interpreted to protect only against involuntary harms. Conduct may be legally regulated to ensure that the exposure to risk is truly voluntary and fully informed. But when it comes to voluntary relationships among consenting adults, liberalism argues that autonomy should be given full sway.

There are still limitations on voluntary transactions imposed on grounds of paternalism, community moral standards, or some other objective notion of harm, to be sure. But they come under relentless assault in the culture of autonomy. Worker protection laws limiting working hours are still on the books to protect children, but not adult women, as they once did. Narcotic use—even use of so-called "recreational drugs," which means those used by the rich—is still a crime, perhaps because these drugs are seen as physically and psychologically addicting and so their use, by definition, cannot be fully "voluntary." Notice that this argument may soon be used in the fight against smoking, as nicotine is addictive and cigarettes may soon be regulated by the Food and Drug Administration as a "drug delivery device."

The winds of the harm principle in legal and public policy debates blow in many directions. Recently in some policy circles, harm as a violation of negative liberty has been interpreted as paying high insurance premiums, and in the future this will cause more headaches for civil libertarians because the harm principle will be extended as a rationale to use coercion to curb risky behaviors that drive up everybody's costs. The insurance system confounds John Stuart Mill's distinction between other-regarding and purely self-regarding behavior. Corporations will soon begin to take a greater interest in the health-related behaviors and characteristics of their employees—diet, exercise, smoking, genetic makeup—in order to hold down their insurance costs as determined by various risk rating and underwriting standards. This poses a substantial threat to the privacy and autonomy of large numbers of individuals in the coming years, and so will be of major concern to civil libertarians. But it will be justified, as all abridgments of freedom must be, on the basis of protecting the rights of healthy, well-behaved, and genetically well-endowed employees against the costly profligacy and self-abuse of those who get sick and drive up health care costs. The very same arguments will be made in the public sphere to protect the interests of taxpayers, who must bankroll the Medicare and Medicaid systems.

The harm principle and negative liberty are rather drafty bulwarks against some quite intrusive forms of state action and social control if they are sufficiently motivated by powerful groups and vested interests in society. Nowhere is a titanic clash between powerful interests more apparent or more interesting than in the smoking wars.

Harm to Others: Blue Smoke and Mirrors

If you want to see the themes, icons, and images of autonomy vividly and graphically on display, you need look no farther than commercial cigarette advertising. Indeed, ever since tobacco was first brought back to Europe from the New World in the sixteenth century, it has been condemned for its moral or social effects and has been appealing to its users precisely as a way of thumbing one's nose at social norms. In recent times, whether it is communicated through the masculine appeal of the Marlboro Man riding unfettered through the Big Sky country, or the chic urban feminism of the smart young woman being reassured that, "You've come a long way, baby," there has been a concerted attempt to associate tobacco use with precisely those feelings and self-images of independence and nonconformity that give us so much satisfaction. These images are no less satisfying—and no less addicting—than smoking itself. They may be just as costly to society, as well. At the very least, smoking is a reliable barometer of the rise and fall of the claims of personal autonomy relative to the claims of others not to be harmed or intruded upon. There is an old saying, "Your freedom ends where my nose begins." With smoking this is literally true.

Some remarkable things have been happening to that barometer. Since 1991 the freedom to smoke in most public places has been drastically restricted or eliminated altogether. Workplace smoking bans have been adopted by federal government agencies and state governments and in hundreds of city and county ordinances throughout the country. Such bans affect not only workplaces but also airports, restaurants, and shopping malls. A tough ordinance in New York City will ban smoking in public access places that are hardly confined or lacking in ventilation, such as Yankee Stadium. In less than a decade, America has moved very rapidly through a series of different types of social accommodations to individual smoking. These amount to different relationships between autonomy —in which the individual makes his own rules and others essentially accommodate themselves to those rules—and social coercion—in which collective rules are made and then imposed on all individuals, backed up by some kind of public sanction or punishment if the individual does not comply voluntarily.

As recently as the early 1980s, smoking in the workplace and in most public places was essentially the individual's decision. Others might complain to the smoker and ask him to refrain, and polite smokers might do so, or else the smokers and nonsmokers would move apart from each other. Civility, mutual adjustment, and mutual inconvenience were the means of public interaction, taking place against the background assumption that the freedom of the individual to smoke was more important than the inconvenience to the nonsmoker. Today, by contrast, informal mutual adjustment has largely been replaced by formal rules and laws. The nonsmoker doesn't have to walk away or move to another seat, and less and less are assertive nonsmokers inclined to do so. They can and do call the manager or the policeman, who, in turn, has the legal authority to order the smoker to stop smoking right then and there. The "In Your Face" society is also a "Get Out of My Face" society.

Most people have taken this transformation so much in stride (and most of them approve of it since they aren't smokers and don't like the smell anyway) that they haven't stopped to notice what a stunning social revolution this actually has been. About 50 million adults—one out of four Americans—smoke, and most are thought to be addicted to it. I cannot think offhand of a similar example in which a behavior that is so important to such a large number of people has so rapidly become socially stigmatized and condemned with the coercive force of law.

In fact, the only equally rapid transformations in significant social mores I can think of go in precisely the opposite direction—public nudity, premarital sex, divorce, childbearing out of wedlock, vulgar or obscene speech, graphic violence in the media, and other aspects of the so-called sexual revolution. These behaviors have rapidly become socially acceptable in recent years. People have either become indifferent about the traditional mores that once condemned such conduct or else have come to think that coercive measures should not be used to repress it. Civility and what used to be called "class" aren't worth the candle. Legal penalties, censorship, shunning, and even feelings of public shame and humiliation are no longer thought to be appropriate responses to these behaviors because they have moved out of the realm of public right and wrong and into the realm of private, subjective belief, value, and self-expression. They have moved, that is to say, where smoking once was: into the realm of autonomy.

What forced smoking out of that realm? Harm to others. In the early 1990s, the debate about smoking was recast in terms of the health effects of environmental tobacco smoke (ETS). Several possible health hazards to those nonsmokers who were exposed to ETS were being studied, but by far the most powerful possibility was that exposure to ETS was linked to lung cancer. This was the conclusion reached in the Environmental Protection Agency's report, which was officially released in January 1993 (though the EPA's preliminary conclusions were publicized as early as 1990). Its main conclusion states: "ETS is a human lung carcinogen, responsible for approximately 3,000 lung cancer deaths annually in U.S. nonsmokers." (U.S. Environmental Protection Agency, *Respiratory Health Effects of Passive Smoking: Lung Cancer and Other Disorders*, Office of Research and Development, Washington, DC. EPA/600/6-90/006F, December 1992, p. 1-1.)

In 1964 the first of many Surgeon's General reports appeared with solid evidence that numerous ingredients in tobacco smoke are carcinogenic and that smoking is correlated with increased risk of several chronic, debilitating, life-threatening diseases. The costs associated with illness, lost work time, and other social expenses related to cigarette smoking have been estimated at approximately $100 billion per year. Billions more have been spent on educational and behavior modification programs, from hypnosis to transdermal nicotine patches. Are these programs cost effective? It is difficult to answer that question, but they clearly have not been as effective as an outright ban on the manufacture and sale of cigarettes would be, or even strict regulation of the ingredients in cigarettes. The political and economic reasons why such a ban has never come about are certainly important; the tobacco industry is a major factor in the economy of some states and regions, and the tobacco lobby has formidable political clout. The federal and state governments themselves rely on the considerable revenues generated by taxes on tobacco products.

In addition to these factors, however, cultural and ideological reasons play an important part too. The political and moral climate of the United States does not permit measures that would significantly restrict smoking behavior as long as smoking is seen as a private choice that affects only the individual adult smoker. This freedom of choice is compatible with health warnings and other information that make the person's choice properly informed. Laws against sale of cigarettes to minors remain on the books, television advertising is banned, and warning labels are mandated by the federal government on all cigarette packages and print advertisements. Although restrictive in certain ways, none of these steps really challenges personal autonomy and freedom of choice. They carefully avoid paternalism. They retain the idea that smoking is a private choice. They nowhere even hint that the freedom of an adult to smoke when one wants and where one wants should be widely or significantly restricted by law.

As a society we are willing to pay an enormous price so that this freedom will not be abridged. An enormous price in terms of the money expended on largely ineffective programs that attempt to discourage smoking without violating the sanctity of freedom of choice, and an enormous price in terms of the sickness and suffering of those who have been granted the freedom to be foolish. Tobacco smoking is responsible for an estimated 434,000 deaths per year, including 112,000 from lung cancer and 156,000 from heart disease. (*Id.*, p. 2-1.)

In the early 1980s, studies comparing the nonsmoking spouses of smokers and nonsmokers began to suggest adverse health effects of exposure to ETS. A decade later, the widely accepted conclusion that ETS causes lung cancer in innocent bystanders became the quintessential argument to curtail the personal autonomy of some individuals (smokers) in order to protect other individuals (nonsmokers) from harm. Smoking where others would be involuntarily exposed to the smoke ceased to be a private choice or self-regarding action and became a public danger. The autonomous right of the smoker to smoke wherever and whenever he chose was trumped by the autonomous right of other people to be free from harmful exposure to ETS. Not merely annoying, obnoxious, or offensive exposure, mind you. And not merely harmful to a relatively small number of people with chronic respiratory conditions, such as asthma. It is unlikely that the legislative wildfire that has swept across the country in the 1990s would have been sustained by harm of this kind. Clearly it was the conclusion reached by the EPA and others about the risk of lung cancer that made the difference. In American society right now, cancer is the mother of all harms. Case closed.

I have already noted that autonomy pushes all moral discourse about the justification of social control into the concept of harm. This has three consequences, none of them good. First, it biases public policy in favor of measures that keep individuals from encroaching upon one another, as distinct from measures that encourage individuals to connect with one another and relate more closely together. Public policy in the liberal state and the culture of autonomy aims to prevent harm, not to promote help.

Next, moral justification in terms of harm tends to turn issues of ethical prescription (or proscription) into issues of factual or scientific description. Defining harm in the first place is a political and philosophical matter, but once it has been defined then the question becomes: Did it in fact occur? To be morally justified and legitimate, coercion (such as anti-smoking laws) based on the harm principle requires scientific evidence that the behavior to be restricted is actually the cause of the harm to be prevented.

The third consequence of basing the moral justification of coercive social policy on the harm principle, therefore, is that it places a terrific ethical and political pressure on scientific research. If a policymaker has a moral reason of a paternalistic or communitarian kind for restricting autonomy, but is afraid that making his case in those terms won't fly, then he will try to gerrymander the argument into the language of harm. But harm must be empirically demonstrated, and science is called upon to step forward and make the case. The risk of politicizing and corrupting scientific research is very real.

This danger works both ways. It can happen when powerful forces want very much to prove that harm exists. It can also happen when such forces want to prove that it does not, or when they do not want to hear that it might. Perhaps the most striking example of this "see no harm, hear no harm" syndrome was the reaction in the late 1960s to a study on the breakdown of the two-parent African-American family conducted by Senator Daniel Patrick Moynihan, who was then a Harvard professor and government advisor. Years later, even leaders of the African-American community would acknowledge that the trends Moynihan documented and the concerns about the effects of this phenomenon that he voiced were valid. But at the time, his work was vilified and largely discredited, at least in liberal circles. Nothing was done to counter the trend that Moynihan tried to warn us of. The children of the Moynihan report are just now coming of age; America is only now beginning to reckon the consequences.

When it comes to smoking and health, warnings of harm are not hushed up, except in secret tobacco company research. The drive to show that ETS exposure causes lung cancer has put pressure on science to prove more than it can. There have been a vast number of studies that show a statistically significant link between cigarette smoking and increased risk of lung cancer in the person who smokes. The average male smoker is twenty times more likely to develop lung cancer than the male nonsmoker; for women the risk ratio is about ten to one. But the EPA report was based on thirty epidemiological studies attempting to find a link between ETS and lung cancer. Of these, only six showed a statistically significant correlation, meaning that the cancer developed by people exposed to ETS was not something caused by random chance. But even these six studies were weak by usual epidemiological standards. The EPA estimated that a woman who lives with a smoker is between one and two times as likely to develop lung cancer as is a woman who lives with a nonsmoker. (Jacob Sullum, "Passive Reporting on Passive Smoke," *Media Critic*, Summer 1994, pp. 41-47.)

This is a very small increase of risk compared with data on active smoking. Increased risks of such a small magnitude might be caused by factors not controlled for in the study, such as diet or exposure to other sources of pollution. Because of this, one cannot confidently conclude that ETS is the cause of lung cancer on the basis of such studies, according to James Enstrom, Professor of Epidemiology at UCLA. "You're talking about ratios that are so close to 1.0 that it's really beyond the realm of epidemiology," Enstrom is quoted as saying. "You could do more studies . . . but as to whether [they] would mean anything, I doubt it . . ." (*Id.*, p. 43.)

Media coverage of the EPA study was largely favorable. More conservative and industry-oriented commentary took a harder line. The periodical *Investor's Business Daily* reported shortly after the EPA report was released that many scientists and policy analysts were critical of the government's conclusions and methodology. Stanton Glantz, an expert on the health effects of smoking at the University of California, San Francisco, defended the EPA methodology and findings: "I review reports like that for the State of California, and the work the EPA did is absolutely first rate, one of the best pieces of science I've seen about anything." But another unnamed public health researcher was quoted as admitting, "Yes, it's rotten science, but it's in a worthy cause. It will help us get rid of cigarettes and become a smoke-free society." (Michael Fumento, "Is EPA Blowing Its Own Smoke?" *Investor's Business Daily*, January 28, 1993, p. 1.)

Rotten science in a worthy cause, if indeed the EPA report is that, is morally and intellectually dishonest. It comes from the arrogance of true believers and their impatient self-righteousness. But it also comes from the narrow forms of moral discourse the culture of autonomy will allow. The concept of harm is crucial and morally indispensable. That is precisely why it should not be abused. It is certainly flexible enough around the edges to adapt to new circumstances and to admit new meanings. Consider, for example, how Kenneth Clark's research on the self-esteem of black children was used in the *Brown v. Board of Education*

Supreme Court case to indicate a kind of psychic harm growing out of "separate but equal" educational systems that had not been clearly recognized for what it was before. Nonetheless, the concept of harm is not infinitely flexible. The meaning of the concept will be destroyed if it is manipulated too readily to accommodate predetermined moral or political conclusions.

In the end, this poses as much of a danger for liberty and autonomy as it does for the intellectual integrity of science. If the morally legitimate and justified authority of the state is to be guided by the harm principle, then public confidence must be maintained in the credibility and the objectivity of at least some experts who are called upon to adjudicate political and moral disagreements. If we politicize scientific research and policy analysis to such an extent that this credibility is lost, the public will be left without any rational basis for deciding whose rights to respect or which policies to support. Or, like the villagers tricked by the boy who cried "wolf," people will grow indifferent to genuine complaints of rights violations by justifiably aggrieved parties and will grow deaf to valid public health, safety, and environmental campaigns.

Unfortunately, America has already gone a long way down this road. Passive exposure to environmental tobacco smoke is not the only (or indeed the most dubious) case, by any means. Largely parallel stories could be told about a host of purported and exaggerated health hazards. DDT, which was more of a danger to birds than to humans, was nonetheless presented as a human health risk to attain the desired conservationist ends. Public fears about asbestos in schools, saccharin, Alar (a chemical used on apples), radon, and many other materials have been deliberately exaggerated and manipulated, and huge sums that surely could have been better spent on other public services and public health projects have been wasted. (Aaron Wildavsky, *But Is It True?: A Citizen's Guide to Environmental Health and Safety Issues*, Harvard University Press, 1995, pp. 26-37; 55-80; 185-222.)

In Pursuit of the Good

In *The Children of Light and the Children of Darkness*, Reinhold Niebuhr makes an observation that helps point us beyond autonomy liberalism and the confines of the harm principle:

"The community requires liberty as much as does the individual; and the individual requires community more than bourgeois thought comprehended. Democracy can therefore not be equated with freedom. An ideal democratic order seeks unity within the conditions of freedom; and maintains freedom within the framework of order." (Charles Scribner's Sons, 1960, p. 3.)

As Niebuhr is using it, the term *democracy* refers, not exclusively to a form of government, but also to a broader social framework and moral outlook. The term *republic* is also sometimes used in this sense. It is a way of life built out of equitable rules and common purposes and out of mutual assistance and respect. It is an environment of cultural meaning and institutional structure that has been considered by a long line of political theorists, beginning with Aristotle, to be the most appropriate setting for the pursuit and the realization of the human good.

Aristotle believed that man is a social and political animal, a *zoon politikon*, and thus destined by nature not for autonomy in the modern sense but for "citizenship." That is, membership in a civic community; life lived as an individual but in the company of equals whom one needs in order to flourish as a human being and by whom one is needed, too. Aristotle characterized the life of citizenship as a kind of alternating current: "ruling and being ruled in turn . . . with a view to attaining a way of life according to goodness." (*Politics*, trans. by Ernest Barker, Oxford University Press, 1971, p. 134.)

I believe that Aristotle was fundamentally right about this. Such a life—the communal, the interdependent life—has a distinctive rhythm. It consists of harmonizing the needs of the self with the claims of others, and the claims of the self with the needs of others. The interdependent life has characteristic vital signs. It is measured by the systole of self-assertion

and the diastole of self-restraint and accommodation—the heartbeat of the body politic. It
consists in the "out-going" of the individual to share
activity and give assistance to others alternating with
the "in-gathering" of the person to refocus one's
unique identity and for a time to dwell within the
self—this constitutes the breathing or spiritual vitality
of the moral community. The human good encompasses
autonomy but is richer, deeper, and more nuanced
than the culture of autonomy understands.

If the moral ideals needed to capture the idea of
the human good as interdependency had to be made
up out of whole cloth—or had to be imported from
some past golden age or some other culture—then we
would truly be in trouble. But they don't. The conception of the good required to moderate the excesses
of the culture of autonomy and contain it within proper
boundaries is close at hand and at our disposal. It is
implicit in our moral common sense, and it is embed-
ded in the lives that the vast majority of ordinary
Americans—and yes, most philosophers too—do in
fact lead. Hobbes advised once and future kings (like
Charles II, whom he hoped would read his book) to
study their own lives and experiences and learn how
to find there the more universal fears and desires of
mankind. In a democracy, each citizen is a mini-sover-
eign and should follow Hobbes's advice. Seek guidance
in the moral sensibilities and the human connections
that are all around us, not in abstract theories or
laboratory experiments. When you think about it, what

could be more logical? Where else would it be better to look?

I will be reminded that America is a heterogeneous and pluralistic society, and so it is. But I believe that liberals have been making a serious mistake in the past few years when they have concluded that this pluralism precludes any serious consideration of the individual or the common good. These liberals think that public moral discourse must be confined to talk of rights and interests, thereby producing what Daniel Callahan, casting a jaundiced eye on it, has aptly called a pervasive "moral minimalism."

I submit, on the contrary, that it is even more important, and probably easier, to have an open, explicit discussion about matters of common interest and social morality in a pluralistic society than it is in a more tightly knit, homogeneous one. African Pygmies, the BaMbuti, don't have to debate abortion, capital punishment, or military conscription. They don't even have to debate whom to marry, how to share, who should hunt and who should gather, or who should do the cooking. (Colin M. Turnbull, *The Forest People*, Simon and Schuster, 1961.) We do. They know where their community and their way of life stand. We don't. Or rather, we can know what we stand for at any given time, but we have to keep working at it, we have to keep arguing. That means we have to engage, and we have to come into conflict. Autonomy as negative liberty—Brandeis's right to be let alone, or Robert Frost's "good fences make good neighbors"—is not enough to sustain a civic community or a way of life in which the human good can flourish. That also means we have to have a moral vocabulary substantive and rich enough to make substantive and subtle arguments with.

An ethic of interdependency highlights several things that the culture of autonomy obscures. In this respect, we can turn to it as a way of enriching the idiom of civic and moral discourse. Interdependency calls attention, first, to human frailty and mortality. Robust, rugged individualism has been America's collective denial of that reality. Every human being will get sick and will die. On that cold piece of granite, any adequate conception of the human good must be anchored. The human good cannot subsist outside a social environment that responds to our condition of need and vulnerability. The culture of autonomy has almost succeeded in convincing Americans that to rely on other people is a bad thing. This is insane. A society that makes it difficult to rely on others is the bad thing.

Second, interdependency reminds us that distinctive individuality, a self of one's own, actually makes no sense apart from, or in opposition to, attachment. Here it is important to distinguish individuality or individuation from individualism. Individuality is a psychological potentiality of human beings and an actual achievement in normal development. Individualism is a prescriptive doctrine that idealizes the person as such, in isolation from others.

It is logically consistent to esteem individuality very highly, while rejecting the doctrine of individualism. Individuality—and this is the critical point—can only arise out of the right kind of human interactions, relationships, and commitments. This is the case from the very beginning where the child gradually attains a distinct identity out of an oscillation of separation and attachment. And it continues throughout adult life, for the process of identity formation is both perpetually unfinished and inextricably social.

Moreover, this side of the Bonanza Hills, we all live in a society marked by increasing, not decreasing, interconnection and mutual reliance. Each of our lives are affected by more people than ever before. And we generally need the cooperation of more people than ever to accomplish our tasks and to achieve our goals, even those goals we set for ourselves. This needs no elaborate demonstration; one is reminded of it with every smoggy breath we take, and every time we step on an airplane and ponder how our life depends on the competent, attentive behavior of dozens of strangers—from the pilot to the air traffic controller to the ground mechanic who was supposed to inspect the extent of the metal fatigue on the wings. Technology increases the links that tie people together, voluntarily or not, and the complexity of our economic system and the organizations we work for multiplies these linkages.

What can autonomy as self-mastery or self-sovereignty possibly mean under such circumstances? One thing is clear: Whatever self-mastery means today, it cannot be thought of as something that a person can achieve on his or her own. That sounds paradoxical, but it isn't really. To exercise control over what happens to you as an individual, you must be involved with others in a process that decides what happens to you and your fellow citizens collectively. We can no longer separate the quality of personal life from the quality of social life. To preserve private space, we must also preserve the commons.

That is one reason why, even in a society so seduced by and attached to autonomy, many people are now getting fed up with what can only be called acts of vandalism against the public space. Threatening, disrespectful, wanton, and manifestly selfish acts—from the warfare of the crack dealers and gangs to the shameless greed of the S&L thieves or the junk bond kings of the 1980s—are poisonous to everyone, and not only to those who are directly harmed or affected by them.

Individual self-mastery is meaningless unless we also have (or can regain, for to a great extent it has been lost) collective or civic self-mastery. Private autonomy and active democratic citizenship have been put at odds by a liberalism that understands citizenship mainly in terms of personal rights, protections, and guarantees. Liberalism has forgotten that citizenship also imposes civic obligations and requires civic virtues. Civic virtues are in fact the traits of character that make one effective in cooperative and collaborative activity and make one at once self-respecting and respectful of others.

Appreciating the role human interdependency plays in the good life for individuals and the ethically good society provides a guiding orientation when balancing autonomy and social control. A society should be so arranged that it responds to the needs and vulnerability of its members. It should protect each person from violence and exploitation. It should actively promote mutual assistance and socially beneficial cooperation. It should give its members equal protection of the laws and a hospitable culture of equal concern and respect. Public policy should sustain institutions that make it possible for people to make the best use of their interdependent condition—to make shared moral life self-fulfilling and beneficial for each person as an individual. And policies should reform institutions and counteract concentrations of power that impede this activity.

Especially crucial are the institutions of socialization and character formation—the family, parenting activities, and educational activities, both formal and informal. These institutions create what the ancient Greeks called *paideia*. By this they meant the moral climate or temperament of the entire society, the well from which each individual drinks to sustain his principled moral commitments, and the underground spring from which each person draws her prereflective habits and conscience by osmosis. Without the institutions of socialization, no civilization or moral order can reproduce itself; no living tradition can be passed on. No appropriate provision for interdependency will be made by adults unless we are able to rear children with the capacities and motivation to carry on this vocation. However crucial it is in the relationship between the individual and the state, autonomy must not be revered so highly that it is allowed to contribute to the unraveling of these institutions.

Re-imagining Freedom, Remembering Society

Our society stands poised between two compelling moral visions. One is the deeply moving transformation of her human being that Baby Suggs experienced when she finally felt the gravity of autonomy and the meaning of being a person in herself and for herself. The other is the promise of civic community and mutuality that courses through the Western political tradition from its ancient Greek origin.

We all stand poised there, and perhaps that is not such a bad place to be. I am firm in my belief that these two visions can hold together, and that the requisite social and moral imagination is available in contemporary America to sustain the proper balance and symbiosis between them.

Indeed, Toni Morrison, among others, provides us with precisely that morally enabling act of mind that is so vital at the present time. The passage concerning Baby Suggs' first experience of freedom, which I singled out to capture one meaning of autonomy, powerful as it is, does not represent the entire message to be found in *Beloved*.

Baby Suggs' daughter-in-law, Sethe, became separated from her husband, Halle, when they were effecting an escape from their owners, and they both went through unspeakable ordeals. Halle witnessed his wife being violated while he lay hidden and dared not move. Sethe, pregnant at the time of her escape, delivered as she made her way toward Ohio and freedom and was helped through her labor by a young white girl she had never seen before. She reached the river with her newborn girl and finally reunited with Baby Suggs and her other children who had been sent on ahead. Halle was captured and killed, although Sethe did not learn that until years later.

Even in Ohio, the family lived in fear. When a party of men came from the South hunting runaway slaves, Sethe hid with her children. When she thought she was going to be discovered and returned to slavery, Sethe, deranged with terror and panic, killed her infant daughter rather than have her grow up enslaved. The local authorities did not permit the bounty hunters to take the family, and Sethe was legally excused for what she had done.

Several years later, her sons grown and gone, her surviving daughter growing up, and Baby Suggs passed away, Sethe is visited by a strange young girl called Beloved, who moves into the house and begins to have an eerie effect on the family. Beloved is in fact the ghost of the murdered infant, and she haunts Sethe by gradually pulling Sethe further and further away from her other human contacts—her daughter, Denver; Paul D, a former slave from Sweet Home plantation who comes to visit and help; and friends in the black community of the small Ohio town. Slowly, the ghost pulls Sethe away from the human world and toward her own hungry spirit, where Sethe will be submerged and enslaved as powerfully as she had been years before, although in a different way.

In one sense, *Beloved* is a story about the second rescue and the second emancipation of Sethe. The ghost nearly succeeds in driving her lover, Paul D, and Denver away, and the stories of a haunting at Sethe's home effectively alienate her fearful neighbors and friends. In a climactic scene, the community gathers in front of the house to urge Sethe to break free of Beloved and return to the human world. Beloved grows menacing, threatening to kill. Sethe makes her choice, again, and joins the company of the living. Beloved disappears. Morrison describes the scene from Beloved's point of view:

"Standing alone on the porch, Beloved is smiling. But now her hand is empty. Sethe is running away from her, running, and she feels the emptiness in the hand Sethe has been holding. Now she is running into the faces of the people out there, joining them and leaving Beloved behind. Alone. Again. Then Denver, running too. Away from her to the pile of people out there. They make a hill. A hill of black people, falling. And above them all, rising from his place with a whip in his hand, the man without skin, looking. He is looking at her." (*Beloved*, p. 262.)

For Beloved, the people Sethe runs toward have no inner structure or connecting sinew; they are merely a collection of separate individuals, a pile, a hill. From the novelist's perspective, and finally from Sethe's too, they are a community of care, concern, and love. They are able to care for one another because they are free. When they were slaves, of course, they could help one another, tend one another, have all the universal human emotions of sympathy, compassion, tenderness, and love. But they couldn't engage in the structured activity of caring and responding *as a community* because the mind-forged, law-forged, and whip-forged manacles of slavery deprived them of the circumstances necessary to make their own community. Freedom makes community possible. But taking care of each other, being a person in the fabric of such a community, is what gives freedom its point. Freedom and commitment, independence and dependence, rights and restraints—these are not, in the final reckoning, contraries. Learning this with more than her mind,

with her whole being, is the difficult road Sethe has
to walk. Morrison's description of Sethe's first
experience of freedom forms an instructive comparison with that of Baby Suggs. Sethe is speaking to
Paul D, with whom she can be uncharacteristically
open about her feelings:

> "I did it. I got us all out. Without Halle too. Up
> till then it was the only thing I ever did on my
> own. Decided. And it came off right, like it was
> supposed to. We was here. Each and every one of
> my babies and me too. I birthed them and I got
> em out and it wasn't no accident. I did that. I had
> help, of course, lots of that, but still it was me
> doing it; me saying, *Go on*, and *Now*. Me having
> to look out. Me using my own head. But it was
> more than that. It was a kind of selfishness I
> never knew nothing about before. It felt good.
> Good and right. I was big, Paul D, and deep and
> wide and when I stretched out my arms all my
> children could get in between. I was *that* wide.
> Look like I loved em more after I got here. Or
> maybe I couldn't love em proper in Kentucky
> because they wasn't mine to love. But when I got
> here, when I jumped down off that wagon—there
> wasn't nobody in the world I couldn't love if I
> wanted to. You know what I mean?" (*Id.*, p.
> 162.)

It is interesting and apt that Morrison should choose the word *selfishness* here and use it without, insofar as I can detect, the slightest hint of a negative moral connotation. It is not the selfishness of taking or grasping; it is the capacity to embrace and draw in. Ordinary, garden-variety selfishness makes one small; this experience of freedom made Sethe big—as big and deep and wide as Christ on the Cross: ". . . when I stretched out my arms all my children could get in between."

Here is a freedom fit for human beings, a freedom consonant with social and moral limits. Here is a freedom that takes our social being seriously and gives choosing value because it gives us something valuable to choose. Here is what the culture of autonomy has forgotten and what moral common sense in America still has the vitality to remember.

Portions of this essay draw upon the author's forthcoming book, coauthored with Willard Gaylin, entitled, *The Perversion of Autonomy*, to be published by the Free Press in 1996.